Notes and Comments on *Robert's Rules*

Notes and Comments on
ROBERT'S RULES

FOURTH EDITION

Jim Slaughter, Gaut Ragsdale, Jon Ericson

Southern Illinois University Press
Carbondale and Edwardsville

Copyright © 1991, 2004, 2012 by the Board of Trustees,
Southern Illinois University
All rights reserved. Second edition 1991.
Third edition 2004. Fourth edition 2012
Printed in the United States of America

15 14 13 12   4 3 2 1

The first edition was published in 1982 as *Motion by
Motion: A Commentary on Parliamentary Procedure.*

Library of Congress Cataloging-in-Publication Data
Slaughter, Jim, 1964–
Notes and comments on Robert's rules / Jim Slaughter,
Gaut Ragsdale, and Jon Ericson. — 4th ed.
    p. cm.
Includes bibliographical references and index.
ISBN-13: 978-0-8093-3215-1 (pbk. : alk. paper)
ISBN-10: 0-8093-3215-9 (pbk. : alk. paper)
ISBN-13: 978-0-8093-3216-8 (ebook)
ISBN-10: 0-8093-3216-7 (ebook)
1. Parliamentary practice. I. Ragsdale, Gaut, 1950– II. Er-
icson, Jon L., 1936– III. Ericson, Jon L., 1936– Notes and
comments on Robert's rules. IV. Title.
JF515.E76 2012
060.4'2—dc23   2012010551

Printed on recycled paper. ♻
The paper used in this publication meets the minimum requirements of American National Standard
for Information Sciences—Permanence of Paper for
Printed Library Materials, ANSI Z39.48-1992. ∞

Contents

Quick-reference charts of parliamentary motions are at the back of the book.

Preface to the Fourth Edition

Notes and Comments on "Robert's Rules" was first published in 1982 under the title *Motion by Motion: A Commentary on Parliamentary Procedure*. In 1991 and 2004, revised editions were published under the present title.

This edition calls attention to substantive changes in the 11th edition of *Robert's Rules of Order Newly Revised* (published 2011), includes new sections, expands the number of questions and answers, updates references and page numbers, and surveys current research in and commentary on the field of parliamentary procedure. *Notes and Comments* is not intended to provide an analysis of every change in the most recent edition of *Robert's*. Listings of such changes can be found in the introduction to the new *Robert's* as well as at the official *Robert's Rules of Order* Web site.

In print for thirty years through three editions, *Notes and Comments* has earned the right to live. It also deserves to be made better. To that end, this fourth edition reflects the contributions of coauthors Jim Slaughter and Gaut Ragsdale, nationally recognized parliamentarians. Jim is an attorney, certified professional parliamentarian, professional registered parliamentarian, and past president of the American College of Parliamentary Lawyers. Gaut is a certified professional parliamentarian, registered parliamentarian, and associate dean and professor at Northern Kentucky University, where he has taught parliamentary procedure.

Because the phrase "Robert's Rules" frequently appears in the title of books on parliamentary procedure, some who buy these books believe they are purchasing the official *Robert's Rules*. Whatever the book or title, sooner or later, like Rome, all roads lead to the 716-page manual, *Robert's Rules of Order Newly Revised* (11th edition). This is where *Notes and Comments* goes to work.

Jon Ericson

Introduction

Organizations that need a parliamentary authority typically adopt *Robert's Rules of Order Newly Revised*. While *Robert's*[1] serves with distinction in this role, it can also intimidate members.

Complaints about the complicated and archaic aspects of parliamentary law have long prompted cries for simplification.[2] The pleas have not fallen on deaf ears. In fact, so many books, booklets, charts, manuals, and articles have been written that one author was moved to begin, "There are hundreds of books about parliamentary procedure. Surely there can be no valid reason for another."[3] Generally, though, these efforts have made little impact on the public not because the attempts to simplify are inadequate but because they are not *Robert's*.[4]

Recent books on parliamentary procedure generally fit into two categories. The first are introductions to the procedures for meetings and are intended as an alternative to reading *Robert's*. In contrast, *Notes and Comments* emphasizes the simple machinery in *Robert's*, relates *Robert's* to the procedures most commonly used in meetings, and elaborates on concepts found in *Robert's* in an easy to follow question-and-answer format. *Notes and Comments* encourages members to obtain and study, rather than avoid, *Robert's Rules of Order Newly Revised*.

The second type of book encourages simple rules as a replacement for formal procedure, generally focusing on the small board, committee, or informal group.[5] The impression is left that larger membership meetings and conventions operate under incomprehensible rules. Few books assist members of such organizations, who can be overwhelmed and threatened by the size and apparent complexity of the rules. *Notes and Comments* is not a replacement for the predominant manual in parliamentary law but is intended to supplement it for participants—those who attend meetings and conventions. *Notes and Comments* addresses the procedures specific to larger assemblies, such as annual meetings and conventions, and suggests where modifications to *Robert's* practices might help. In addition, *Notes and*

Comments provides commentary on and comparisons with other major parliamentary authorities, especially in the notes. The premise of *Notes and Comments* is that parliamentary procedure should enable members to achieve their objectives rather than intimidate them,

On *Robert's Rules*

Robert's Rules of Order was first published in 1876; the first major revision, *Robert's Rules of Order Revised,* appeared in 1915. Throughout the 1960s, hopes for a modern and simplified *Robert's* were heightened by the knowledge that a second major revision was under way.

It was not to be. *Robert's Rules of Order Newly Revised* appeared in 1970 as a significantly expanded work (almost doubling in size). One reviewer, Marshall Soren, began, "The long heralded and long awaited new revision of *Robert's Rules of Order . . .* is, in many ways, extremely well done. Yet, a sigh of regret is . . . appropriate, for the book is painfully out of date."[6] After praising the thoroughness of the book, the writing style, and the organization, Soren complained, "it is reasonable to expect authors to use the English language as it is understood today," and added, "but there is a worse problem in the book than the retention of obsolete language, and that is the retention of obsolete and awkward concepts. Many motions discussed in the volume are either unused or unnecessary for modern practice."[7]

Speaking for the leadership of the American Institute of Parliamentarians, Emogene Emery praised the 1970 edition for "organization, the style and lucidity of the writing, the clarity of the charts, its additional explanation and illustration," but she too expressed disappointment that the "terminology had not been modernized" and "the rules had not been simplified."[8] Others joined in the lament that *Robert's* had been neither modernized nor simplified.[9]

The authors of the revision had given warning, prior to publication, not to expect a *Robert's* abridged. Coauthor James W. Cleary had previously stated that a hallmark of the revision would be its "continuing completeness and comprehensiveness" and that it would "not exclude motions or rules on the presumption that infrequent use in certain circles makes them unnecessary."[10] Coauthor William J. Evans flatly stated, "We are not trying to simplify the subject matter," but that instead their edition "aims to be the last word." Lest anyone wonder, he noted that "It is not a novel; it is not designed to be used quickly."[11] Coauthor Henry M. Robert III explained after publication that the intent had been "to develop the subject more fully."[12] Subsequent editions, including the recent 11th Edition, have only increased in size, with the book now at 716 pages. While some practices have been tweaked or wording updated (such as recognizing telephonic or electronic communications), it is clear that the authors are not pushing for simplification any time soon.

Although there may be disappointment for those who wanted *Robert's* simplified, when judged by the intent of the authors, the recent editions of *Robert's* can receive only acclaim. Their charge, as the authors see it, was to preserve and to enhance *Robert's* as the authoritative reference manual and code for meeting procedures. Henry M. Robert III, senior author of the 11th Edition and the grandson of the original author, Henry Martyn Robert, explains: "We feel he transmitted to us the authority to interpret and to a limited degree extend his work, but not to revamp it wholesale."[13] The task of making *Robert's* understandable is left to others. That's the purpose of *Notes and Comments.*

Parliamentary Procedure as Scapegoat

Few of us have much tolerance for the person who sits at the table to play cards or who wanders onto a basketball court who has not first learned the rules of the game. Learning the rules *before* you play goes without saying. Yet, by the thousands, members arrive at meetings without having learned the rules of the game. But why learn *those* rules? After all, isn't parliamentary procedure that tricky, pedantic, officious, dull, boring, unfair system that tyrants use to suppress rights?

Not much learning—and even less joy—can take place when a subject suffers from such a negative attitude. A study of parliamentary procedure, then, must begin by confronting the misconception that allows procedure to serve as a handy scapegoat for our unwillingness to do our homework.

Most of us can recall the frustration of attending meetings and continually failing to understand what is going on. Or worse, suffering parliamentary defeat because our opponents were more adept at procedure. It can get old. It is also easily remedied.

Somewhere along the line, the three of us tired of relying on others for instructions about what could or couldn't be done. So we learned parliamentary procedure. It was surprisingly painless, and the benefits are lifelong. We then knew that, regardless of the meeting or convention, if others were going to defeat us, they would have to have the better argument, or do a better job of getting supporters to the meeting. They wouldn't defeat us because they knew more about parliamentary procedure than we did. And that is a good feeling. Parliamentary procedure is simply another form of power, which should be relinquished by no one. Too many members, armed—or more accurately, disarmed—with a misconception of parliamentary procedure, spend their lives wondering what is going on and lamenting their fate or blaming others for not getting their way.

Understanding meeting procedures also allows a person to enjoy participating in the public arena. Understanding parliamentary procedure opens the door to public performance, and in stepping onto that stage, you may find a once scary and terrifying experience becomes an opportunity to satisfy an inherent need to perform— and the opportunity to have fun.

How to Use This Book

Readers beginning a study of parliamentary procedure should start with Part I, which presents the fundamental concept of parliamentary procedure that must be understood before a study of motions will make sense. Part II addresses the basics of introducing and handling a motion. Part III presents motions that members must understand to be effective members and delegates for their organizations and examines several motions often referred to but seldom used. Part IV explores additional topics in parliamentary procedure that are necessary for efficient meetings and conventions.

The book is written in the question-and-answer format on the premise that most members of organizations turn to a manual on parliamentary procedure only when they are faced with a procedural problem. They do not read to learn about the subject of parliamentary procedure. They read to solve a problem.

Why, then, include notes? The notes take the reader behind the scene to discover not a static code but an evolving process; not a vacuum but a vigorous debate; and most important, to discover that members are not controlled by, but have a choice over, the rules by which they will be bound.

PART I

Ranking of Motions

Order of Precedence

High

Privileged Motions

Fix the Time to Which to Adjourn
Adjourn
Recess
Raise a Question of Privilege
Call for the Orders of the Day

Subsidiary Motions

Lay on the Table
Previous Question (Close Debate)
Limit or Extend Limits of Debate
Postpone to a Certain Time
Refer
Amend
Postpone Indefinitely

Main Motion

Main Motion (or Resolution)

Low

For a more complete list of motions that provides easy, at-a-glance information, see the back-of-the-book charts, also available as a pocket-sized, laminated card.

Order of Precedence

Where does one begin a study of parliamentary procedure?

The basic concept on which parliamentary procedure is built, the concept that underlies the relationship—the ranking—of motions, is called the *order of precedence* (pree-SEED-n's) (58–62).[14] Members are often overwhelmed and ineffective at large meetings and conventions because motions seem to dart in and out like bees around a beehive. Although members (delegates) tend to blame those who are running the convention, as often as not the problem is simply that they do not understand the order of precedence of motions.

Order of precedence tells a member two things: when a motion is in order and in what order to vote on pending motions.

First, the order of precedence tells a member at any given time whether the motion that the member wishes to make is in order. A motion higher in rank than the immediately pending motion (being considered by the body) may be introduced, but a motion lower (or equal) in rank is not in order. To follow the examples below, refer to the list of motions shown in the preceding figure.

- If a main motion is pending, the order of precedence tells a member that it would be in order to move to Amend the main motion because the motion to Amend is *higher* in rank than the main motion.
- If a main motion and a motion to Amend are pending, the order of precedence tells a member that a motion to Refer to committee would be in order because the motion to Refer is *higher* in rank than the motion to Amend.
- If a main motion, a motion to Amend, and a motion to Refer are pending, the order of precedence tells a member that a motion to Recess would be in order because it is *higher* in rank than one to Refer, but a motion to Postpone Indefinitely would not be in order because it is *lower* in rank than a motion to Refer.

Second, the order of precedence tells a member, when it is time to vote, in what order to vote on the pending motions. Motions are voted on in the reverse order from which they were made. Thus, in the previous example, four motions are pending before the body:

Recess
Refer
Amend
Main motion

The first vote is taken on the highest ranking motion (the *immediately pending question*)—the motion to Recess. If the motion to Recess is adopted, the meeting is in recess. If that motion to Recess is rejected, discussion is open on the motion to Refer. If the vote on the motion to Refer is eventually adopted, the entire issue is referred to committee. If the vote on the motion to Refer is rejected, discussion is open again on the motion to Amend. Eventually, a vote will be taken on the motion to Amend. Then discussion is open again on the main motion—either as amended or as originally proposed, depending on the vote on the amendment. The final vote is on the main motion (58–62, 79, 116–18). Prior to the vote on the main motion, other motions may be made, considered, and voted upon, so long as they are *higher* in rank than any pending motion.

Parliamentary motions, then, are handled like children's play blocks: when working upward (making motions), one goes on top of another; when working downward (voting on motions), the top one is taken off first to ensure proper dismantling in orderly fashion. When the members do not adhere to the order of precedence and the bottom block is pulled out of turn, the result is a mess.[15]

PART II

Getting Started: Basic Provisions for Handling a Motion

What is the procedure for obtaining the floor to introduce a motion?

Before making a motion, a member must obtain the floor. To do so, a member rises (or goes to a microphone in larger assemblies) and addresses the chair by title (29, 376–77). In *Robert's*, "The term *the chair* refers to the person in a meeting who is actually presiding at the time, whether that person is the regular presiding officer or not [i.e., president, chairman, speaker, or moderator]" (448). The chair then recognizes the member by announcing the member's name or title. In large conventions, a delegate will state his name and unit represented prior to speaking. Members are not required to rise in smaller boards and committees to be recognized (29, 487).

What are the steps for handling a motion?

There are six steps for handling main motions and other debatable motions. *Robert's* divides them into three steps for bringing forward a motion and three for considering a motion:

1. A member makes the motion by stating, "I move that . . ." (32–33). (Do not say "I make the motion that . . .")
2. Another member seconds the motion by calling out, "Second!" (35).
3. The chair states the motion, "It is moved and seconded that . . ." (37). (Do not say "It *has been* moved and seconded that . . .")
4. Members debate the motion (42).
5. The chair takes the vote (or "puts the question to a vote") (44).
6. The chair announces the result (47).

These steps may vary depending on the parliamentary situation and whether the specific motion is debatable, requires a vote, etc.

May the chair simply place a motion before the body?

Generally, no. However, in instances where members are generally in favor of an action or there seems to be "no opposition in routine business or on questions of little importance," the chair can place the motion before the body without a formal motion (54). An example might be the chair asking, "Is there is any objection to approving the minutes?"

What is the purpose of the second?

The purpose of the second "is to prevent time from being consumed by the assembly's having to dispose of a motion that only one person wants to see introduced" (36). The goal of parliamentary procedure is to balance individual and majority rights. When the organization finds itself with an oddball who wastes valuable time making ridiculous motions, the delicate balance is lost. Thus, the requirement of the second is a fine-tuning device that restores the balance by requiring at least one other member who thinks the motion is worth talking about. (The purpose is admirable—few people argue in favor of wasting time—but alas, most organizations have more than one oddball. There is always the member who will second anything.)

What if the chair forgets to ask for a second?

Prior to debate, a member may raise a Point of Order that the motion has not received a second. But concern for the second is often overdone. Even *Robert's* advises: "In handling routine motions, less attention is paid to the requirement of a second. If the chair is certain that a motion meets with wide approval but members are slow in seconding it, he can state the question without waiting for a second" (36–37).

Robert's advice is well taken because three misconceptions result from excessive concern about a second. The first misconception is that a motion is out of order if it is discovered during debate that the motion was not seconded. Once debate has begun, a motion is not out of order if it was not seconded. Recall that the rationale for requiring a second is to ensure that at least one other member thinks the motion is worth talking about. Once debate has progressed, the rationale has been met (36–37).

The second misconception is that an adopted motion is null and void if it is later discovered that the motion was never seconded. Obviously, if the body adopts a motion, the rationale for requiring a second has been met.

Neither of these two misconceptions will occur, of course, if the chair remembers to obtain a second, but it is not unusual to hear a Point of Order that "This motion was not seconded" turn into a "parliamentary hassle." Typically, the parliamentary procedure, not the members' ignorance, is blamed for the breakdown in the meeting.

The third misconception is that the chair must obtain the permission of the seconder when the maker of the motion requests permission to withdraw or modify it. All members share equally in the ownership of a motion once it has been stated by the chair; therefore, the chair asks for the permission of all members, including the seconder, rather than asking for the permission only of the seconder. Remember, the member who seconds a motion simply thinks the motion is worth discussing. Seconding a motion does not give that member power to grant or deny a request to modify or withdraw the motion.

Do all motions require a second?

No.[16]

Are seconds required in all bodies?

No. Seconds to motions are not required in smaller boards or committees (488, 500). The 11th Edition suggests that smaller assemblies "having a dozen or fewer members" should consider adopting rules similar to those governing small boards, including that no seconds are required (16, 487–88).

Must the seconder be in favor of the motion?

No. A second merely means that the seconder thinks that the motion should come before the body (36).

Is it necessary to be recognized (obtain the floor) to second a motion?

No (35). Much time is wasted in meetings while a member goes to the microphone to second a motion. The name of the seconder does not even go in the minutes (470).

Must a second be in a certain form?

No, anything that informs the chair that another member wishes the motion to come before the meeting is sufficient. As a result, "Second!,"

"I second the motion," "I second it," or even "Support" (used in some unions) is sufficient (35).

Could an organization eliminate the requirement of a second for all motions?

Yes, several authorities argue that the requirement of a second should be abolished.[17] To avoid the misconceptions, complications, and time involved in requiring a second, an organization may adopt a special rule: motions shall not require a second. Such a rule works best for smaller bodies; in fact, some large convention rules require multiple seconds or a fixed number of delegates, such as fifty, to introduce a motion.[18]

When a motion is open to debate, what guidelines should the chair follow in directing debate?

1. The maker of the main motion must be recognized first. This act is not only a courtesy but also provides for the affirmative to assume the burden of proof (34, 42, 379).

2. Members who have not yet spoken must be recognized before other members are allowed to speak a second time (31, 43). No member has the right to speak a second time until every member has had the opportunity to speak.

3. Debate should alternate between pro and con (31). The 11th Edition adds language to facilitate this, such as "Since the last speaker spoke in favor of the motion, who wishes to speak in opposition to the motion?" (31).

May a speaker yield his or her time?

No, rights in regard to debate are not transferable without a special rule (388).

May the maker of a motion speak against his or her motion?

No. A maker who no longer likes the motion may request permission to withdraw it (393). (See "Voting," page 127.)

On occasion, the prohibition against speaking against one's motion conflicts with the advice in *Robert's* "to avoid a motion containing a negative statement" (105).[19] There can be circumstances in which a motion must be proposed by someone who wishes it to fail. For instance, a motion that a teacher be granted tenure might be proposed by someone opposed to the teacher as an alternative to a motion "not to grant tenure." Similarly, some contracts require that a vote must be taken on extending the agreement. Rather than proposing that the contract "not be extended," a member will move that the agreement be extended, in hopes the motion will be defeated. In such instances, the maker of the motion wants to speak against the motion, which is prohibited in *Robert's*. Some authorities permit a maker to speak against the motion because, as stated in *The Standard Code*, 4th edition, "it is unfair to deny anyone an opportunity to express an opinion simply because the person initially held a different opinion."[20]

May a nonmember debate a motion?

No. Meetings are for members. With that said, statutes, governing documents, or specific rules can change this general principle.[21] For instance, members of the public are often permitted to address governmental bodies, such as school boards. Or, members of a community association may be permitted to speak at board meetings, even though they are not board members. Similarly, union members may sometimes speak on issues at a convention, even if they are not delegates. Without higher authority overriding *Robert's*, however, only members of the assembly addressing an issue may participate (96–97).

How should the chair put a voice vote to the assembly? (Or, what error does the chair often make when taking a voice vote?)

The chair states, "Those in favor of the motion, say 'Aye.' Those opposed, say 'No'" (45). (Do not say "All those in favor" or "All those who are in favor . . ." Keep it clean: "Those in favor . . .") Many chairs make the mistake of saying "Those in favor, say 'Aye.' Opposed?" (or even worse, "Those opposed, same sign").[22] When the chair omits the negative cue ("Those opposed, say 'No'"), the negative votes are voiced as a string of "No," "No," "Aye," "No," which deprives members who wish to vote in the negative of the opportunity to vote in unison and thus gives an advantage to the affirmative. (Some voters in the negative say "No" immediately following "Opposed?" Some wait for the cue "say 'No.'" Others say "Aye" in place of "No.") Acting somewhat like an orchestra conductor, the chair must remember: *always give the negative the same cue as the affirmative.* "Say 'No'" may seem like a minor point, but it is not. Members typically become irritated with the chair not because of some major abuse, but due to the sum of many little things. With only a little training in procedure, these little things can be eliminated, and the delegates will return home happy with their leader. So practice repeatedly, "Those opposed, say 'No.'"[23]

What are the chair's responsibilities in announcing a vote?

When announcing the vote, the chair has three responsibilities:

1. report the vote, including an announcement of the count if the vote was taken by count;
2. state whether the motion was adopted or rejected (or "lost" according to *Robert's*); and
3. announce the effect of the vote (48).

The 11th Edition clarifies that part of this announcement includes the chair's stating the next item of business or, if there are other motions pending, "the next motion that consequently comes up for consideration" (49).

When announcing the vote, announce the affirmative vote first. For example, say, "By a vote of four to fourteen the motion is lost [or 'rejected']." Do *not* say "By a vote of fourteen to four, the motion is rejected." For some reason, people often want to give the larger number first. The affirmative vote is always taken first, so it should be announced first. Announcing the affirmative number first may sound like a minor point, but remember, it's the little things.

Putting the three responsibilities together, the chair sounds like this: "By a vote of twenty-five to thirty-seven, the motion to adopt the dues increase is rejected. The next item of business is . . ." Or, "By a vote of fourteen to three, the motion to increase the dues is adopted. The increase will take effect 1 July. We turn now to the report of the membership committee."

Once the assembly is in the mood to conduct business, it is the responsibility of the chair to retain that mood. If the chair stumbles around, wonders aloud what item of business is next, or simply allows time for small discussions to break out, the business mood will be broken, and it is no small task to recapture it.

PART III

Main Motion

Since the main motion brings business before the body, what guidelines should the chair follow when main motions are presented to avoid later difficulties?

First, the chair should not allow debate if there is no main motion pending (34, 114, 376). Unfortunately, new business at times consists of members rising to complain or to draw attention to a particular problem. That may lead to a discussion or gripe session, but business meetings are about taking action. Time is wasted and business will not be expedited if debate is allowed before a main motion is pending. *Robert's* states: "The general rule against discussion without a motion is one of parliamentary procedure's powerful tools for keeping business 'on track,' and an observance of its spirit can be an important factor in making even a very small meeting rapidly moving and interesting" (34–35). In formal procedure, the assembly and the chair are unable to do anything until a main motion is made, so when a member wishes to bring business to the attention of the assembly, his opening words should be, "I move that . . ." (See "The Chair," page 142.)

Second, the chair should insist that the main motion make sense (104–5). Too often, in an effort to be agreeable, the chair allows an unclear motion to be introduced, setting the stage for all kinds of trouble. It is the chair's responsibility to see that the proposer of the main motion states the motion clearly. To assist the maker and to ensure clarity, the chair should state the motion *before* debate is allowed. Restatement of the main motion by the chair not only clarifies the motion but also transfers ownership of the motion from the proposer to the assembly. (See "Modify or Withdraw a Motion," page 95.) An additional protection is to request that complex motions be submitted in writing (33, 101).

How does the chair present a main motion to the assembly?

The chair must state the motion: "It is moved and seconded that . . ." First, stating the motion ensures clarity. Too often the member's motion is vague, poorly worded, and imprecise. By helping the member see the need for changes in the wording and offering suggestions for more precise and appropriate language, the chair can help the process. When there is doubt about the wording of a motion, the motion that the chair states is the official motion.

A paragraph in *Robert's* emphasizes the importance of clarity, clarity, clarity:

> The chair should take special care to make sure that the members always understand what is the immediately pending business—the *exact* question to be voted on the next time a vote is taken. Failure of presiding officers to do so is one of the greatest causes of confusion in meetings. . . . It is far better to risk taxing the patience of an assembly by repeating the wording of a motion on which all may be clear, than to risk taking a vote whose effect may be unclear to even a few members. (454–55)

Second, stating the motion transfers ownership of the motion from the maker to the assembly (40, 114). Thus, "It is moved and seconded that . . ." is one of the first phrases that should be drummed into the head of every chair.

What main motions are not in order?

In addition to the requirements that a main motion must make sense and that only one main motion can be pending at a time, *Robert's* lists five conditions under which a main motion is *not in order*. No main motion is in order that:

1. "conflicts with the corporate charter, constitution, or bylaws . . . [or any] procedural rules applicable to the organization or assembly [that] are prescribed by federal, state, or local law";
2. "presents substantially the same question as a motion that was finally disposed of earlier in the same session by being rejected, postponed indefinitely, or subjected to an Objection to the Consideration of a Question that was sustained";
3. "conflicts with a motion previously adopted at any time and still in force" (other than a motion to Rescind or to Amend Something Previously Adopted);
4. "that would conflict with or that presents substantially the same question as one which has been *temporarily but not finally disposed of* . . . and which remains *within the control of the assembly*"; or,

5. "that proposes action outside the scope of the organization's object as defined in the bylaws or corporate charter" (110–13, 343–44).

Is a motion to reaffirm a main motion previously adopted in order?

No, at times members or delegates want "to send a clear message" that the organization "really means it," or that they believe the leaders haven't carried out a previously adopted motion with sufficient dispatch. Whatever the reason, the delegates feel strongly about the issue, and someone moves to reaffirm. The motion is good therapy, but poor procedure: "Such a motion serves no useful purpose because the original motion is still in effect. . . . If such a motion to reaffirm failed, it would create an ambiguous situation" (104).

Resolution

Is a resolution a main motion?

Yes. Consisting of the optional preamble "Whereas" and the body "Resolved" or "Be it resolved that . . . ," a resolution is the traditional form of an original main motion, and rules relating to the former apply equally to the latter. Both the main motion ("I move that . . .") and a written resolution are proposals for action (105–9).

Must a resolution contain "Whereas" clauses?

Except for commendation, courtesy, or honorary purposes, use of "Whereas" clauses is generally unwise. Why?

1. The traditional form is archaic. Neither rule nor custom requires a resolution to have a preamble (106–7).

2. The traditional form is more complicated than a main motion:

> In the consideration of a resolution having a preamble, the preamble is always amended last, since changes in the resolving clauses may require changes in the preamble. In moving the adoption of a resolution, the preamble is not usually mentioned, since it is included in the resolution. When the *Previous Question* is ordered on the resolution before the preamble has been considered for amendment, however, the *Previous Question* does not apply to the preamble, which becomes open to debate and amendment

unless the *Previous Question* is then separately ordered on it also. (108). (See "Previous Question (Close Debate)," pages 53–58.)

3. The traditional form can work against the adoption of the motion. Some members who approve of the proposed action may vote against the motion because of statements in the preamble (107). For example, a resolution recommending endorsement of one political candidate might be opposed by members who are offended by clauses that criticize other candidates.

On top of all this, according to *The Standard Code*, the preamble has no legal effect on the motion.[24] There are, however, two minor strategic reasons for including a preamble.

1. Since the preamble contains the reasons for adopting the motion, the traditional form allows the assembly to hear the maker's argument before the motion becomes the property of the assembly.[25]

2. Since minutes do not include debate, the preamble preserves the reasons for the action having been taken.

If an annual meeting adopts resolutions that are formal expressions of opinion or philosophy, how long do these resolutions remain in force, and do they have to be acted on at each annual meeting?

Some organizations refer to these expressions of philosophy as "continuing resolutions" (in contrast to regular main motions, which call for specific action), and they may be handled in one of two ways:

1. Continuing resolutions remain in force until action is taken on any or all of them. A main motion would be required to remove ("to strike resolution number . . .") or to change ("to amend resolution number . . .") a continuing resolution. No action is required on resolutions that the delegates wish to "continue."

2. Continuing resolutions are like trophies in a trophy case: every year, each trophy is taken out of the case, dusted, checked, and a decision made about whether to put it back in the case. The resolutions continue only if the delegates adopt them (put them back in the case) every year.

Organizations often prefer the second approach because it suggests an annual review of the organization's philosophical positions.

Does annual review of continuing resolutions mean that each continuing resolution must be considered individually by the delegates?

No, not separately.

What is the most efficient method for an assembly to handle a large number of resolutions?

The chair states, "The assembly has before it the report of the resolutions committee containing _____ resolutions. The procedure is as follows: all resolutions will be considered as a single motion except for those resolutions that the assembly wishes to consider separately. Members who wish to have a resolution considered separately will be asked to state, 'Hold [Set aside] resolution _____.' All resolutions not held [not set aside] will be voted on as a package. Then, each resolution placed on hold will be considered separately. Are there any requests to place a resolution on hold?"

This procedure, which is a form of dividing the question, expedites the business of the assembly (274–75); at the same time, it protects the rights of the minority—the delegate who wishes to have the assembly consider one of the resolutions. (See "Committees," pages 40–41, for how a committee functions as a clearinghouse for new or continuing resolutions.)

Postpone Indefinitely

What is the purpose of the motion to Postpone Indefinitely?

The motion suppresses action and kills the main motion for the duration of that meeting (63, 126). The purpose is *not* to postpone the main motion. Postpone Indefinitely provides a way to avoid taking a position on the main question.

If a member is against the main motion, why not simply vote against it?

One would usually vote against the main motion rather than move to postpone indefinitely. On occasion, however, the assembly may not wish to go on record as voting either for or against the main motion. "It is useful in disposing of a badly chosen main motion that cannot be either adopted or expressly rejected without possibly undesirable consequences" (126).

An example of this might be where a motion has been made to honor a beloved member of an organization with a distinguished award soon after her death, but the member does not meet the criteria for the award. Rather than vote down the motion, Postpone Indefinitely could be used. Or when a motion has been made before a school board to ban junk food from school premises and school-related functions, but upon hearing arguments that the motion would adversely affect fund-raising activities (e.g., money for band uniforms), members of the board want to defeat the motion without appearing to vote in favor of junk food. Postpone Indefinitely provides the board with a method of effectively killing the motion without voting in favor of junk food.[26] In other words, Postpone Indefinitely allows an assembly to kill the motion without voting on the motion itself.

In addition, there are two strategic purposes of the motion to Postpone Indefinitely.

1. The motion to Postpone Indefinitely opens the main motion to debate; therefore, if a member has used up her debating time on the main motion, she can move to postpone it indefinitely and in effect

speak again on the main motion (127). Similarly, a quickly made motion to Postpone Indefinitely may allow a member to debate the issue prior to debate on the main motion. Recall *Robert's* limitation on debate: a member may speak twice on the same motion on the same day for no longer than ten minutes at a time (43, 388–89).

2. If a member is against the main motion, a vote on postponing indefinitely provides a straw vote without the risk of having the main motion adopted (128). (See "Voting," page 129 for why a straw vote should not be allowed.)

Why does the motion to Postpone Indefinitely reopen the main motion to debate? Isn't debate restricted to the immediately pending motion?

Technically, "debate must be confined to the merits of the pending question" (43). However, the reasons in favor of postponing indefinitely become the reasons against the adoption of the main motion; the reasons against postponing indefinitely are usually the reasons in favor of the main motion. *Robert's* says, "Unlike the case of any other subsidiary motion, debate on the motion to *Postpone Indefinitely* can go fully into the merits of the main question" (127).

If the motion to Postpone Indefinitely is adopted, for how long is the main motion dead?

The main motion is dead for the duration of the session at which it is killed. It can be made again at the next session. However, if a member voted with the majority to kill the main motion, he could move to Reconsider the vote on the motion to Postpone Indefinitely (127). (See "Reconsider," pages 101–4.)

Why is the motion to Postpone Indefinitely seldom used?

The motion to Postpone Indefinitely is seldom used because

1. it is low in precedence—it cannot be made when a subsidiary or privileged motion is pending;

2. opponents of the main motion simply speak and vote against the main motion; and

3. the motion to Lay on the Table is misused as a motion to kill the main motion. (See "Lay on the Table," page 60.)

Postpone Indefinitely is rarely used primarily because few members are aware of or understand the purpose of the motion. The fault may be that the motion is misnamed. As stated earlier, the purpose is not to postpone the main motion. This confusing characteristic could be corrected, of course, by renaming the motion *the motion to kill* or *the motion to decline to take a position on the main motion* or, as some parliamentary authorities suggest, simply eliminate the motion.

Should the motion to Postpone Indefinitely be used more often?

Parliamentary authorities differ. The traditionalists say that there are occasions when the motion helps an organization avoid going on record on an embarrassing main motion. So do your homework and learn the rules.

Many contemporary authorities argue that it is fortunate that the motion is seldom used because the strategic uses of the motion contribute to parliamentary procedure's reputation as being manipulative and confusing and are inconsistent with other parliamentary rules. Also, on the rare occasion when the assembly needs to avoid a vote on a main motion, other means are available. For example, the maker of the motion can be urged to request permission to withdraw the motion. The assembly can move to refer the question to committee. The assembly can postpone the motion to follow the last item of business and then adjourn prior to taking a vote on the main motion.[27]

Our view? We come down firmly on both sides. The motion is not the monster its critics make it out to be (read ahead for some that are worse), but a member can certainly serve with distinction without ever using the motion to Postpone Indefinitely.

Then again, it never hurts to know more than you need to know.

Amend (the Amending Process)

How can the chair know if a motion is amendable?

In the absence of memorizing whether each motion is amendable, a good guideline to apply is that a motion is amendable if it is variable in wording (132). A main motion, for example, is amendable because it is variable in wording, but the motion to Postpone Indefinitely is not amendable because it is not variable in wording.

How does a member proceed in making an amendment?

There are three ways to amend:

1. Insert or add.
2. Strike.
3. Strike and insert words or substitute (133–34).

Actually, *Robert's* says "strike out" words—although in a note it says, "the shortened expression 'to strike' is acceptable" (134). We like "strike." "Strike out" is redundant. "I move to *strike*" has a cleanness to it, a rapier-like sharpness, a thrust into the motion of which opponents ought to beware.

It is in the amending process where many meetings become confusing. Too often, makers of motions to Amend ramble rather than discipline themselves to one of the three ways listed. The chair should insist that members be concise with respect to the words they choose to use in their amendments. Members should say what is to be struck, then what is to be inserted, and nothing more.

Some well-intentioned members think they are helping to clarify by stating, "I move to amend so the motion will read . . ." Do not do this. Everyone now has to search through the motion to locate which specific words are being inserted or added, struck, or struck and inserted. *After* the chair states the specific proposed change and members can see the proposed change, then the chair can inform the members or delegates how the motion will read if the amendment is adopted.

Generally, amendments should be submitted in writing; and, as with the main motion, it is important that the chair state the amendment before allowing any debate.

What is meant by *germane*?

"Germane" means relevant to, that is, "closely related to or having bearing on the subject of the motion to be amended" (131, 136–38). Amendments must be germane.

How can one be sure an amendment is germane?

The distinction is not always easy. One must examine the context of the motion to reach a decision. Consider, for example, the main motion, "I move that we recognize Professor Adams as the outstanding teacher at the university."

If the intent of the motion is to get the organization to express its feelings about Professor Adams, then

1. an amendment to strike "outstanding teacher" and insert "big windbag" would be in order;

2. an amendment to strike "Professor Adams" and insert "Professor Wilson" would not be in order.

If the intent of the motion is to select the recipient for the organization's outstanding teacher award, then

1. an amendment to strike "outstanding teacher" and insert "big windbag" would not be in order;

2. an amendment to strike "Professor Adams" and insert "Professor Wilson" would be in order.

An amendment may be hostile to the specific intent of the motion as long as it is germane to the general intent of the motion.[28]

What is meant by a *hostile amendment*?

Robert's states that "an amendment can be hostile to, or even defeat, the spirit of the original motion and still be germane" (136). Take, for example, the motion "that the executive director be given a thirty-day paid vacation." It would be in order for a member to move to strike "paid vacation" and insert "notice." Why? The amendment certainly changes the maker's intent to do something nice for the executive director, but the amendment is relevant to the general intent of the motion, which is for the organization to express its opinion of the executive director. Remember, once the motion becomes the property of the body, all members share in the ownership of the motion; therefore, any member has the right to present a specific opinion about the proposal as long as the amendment is relevant (germane) to the general intent of the motion. The proposer of the amendment has the same right to say something bad (hostile) about the executive director as the maker of the main motion has to say something nice. The key, then, is to distinguish between the specific intent and the general intent of a motion.

What is the difference between the motion to Amend and the motion to Amend the amendment?

The motion to Amend is a primary amendment (first degree), which modifies the immediately pending motion; the motion to Amend the amendment is a secondary amendment (second degree), which modifies a pending primary amendment. There is no such thing as a third-degree amendment. (For an effect similar to what would be a third-degree amendment, see "Create a Blank," pages 31–33.) For example, reading from the bottom upward:

> I move to amend the amendment by striking "two" and inserting "four." [Secondary Amendment]
> I move to amend the motion by adding "and allow each member to invite two guests." [Primary Amendment]
> I move that we have an awards ceremony next month. [Main Motion]

(Technically, of course, a secondary amendment is just an amendment. However, because the amending process can be confusing, in the pocket-sized chart we have inserted the second-degree amendment into the order of precedence. Doing so reminds the chair—and members—of the difference, procedurally, between primary and secondary amendments.)

Is there a limit to the number of amendments that can be made?

No. There is no limit to the number of amendments to a motion as long as there is only one amendment of the same rank on the floor at a time.

What limitations affect the amending process?

Only one amendment of the same degree can be on the floor (pending) at a time. Recall the difference between primary and secondary amendments (see above); and recall that, according to the order of precedence (see "Order of Precedence," page 3), a motion is in order only if it is higher in precedence than the immediately pending motion.

If an amendment is proposed to a motion that requires more than a majority vote for its adoption (e.g., two-thirds vote), what vote is required to adopt the amendment?

An amendment requires a majority vote regardless of the vote required for the original motion (133).

Is the motion to Amend always debatable?

No, the motion to Amend is not debatable whenever the motion to be amended is not debatable. The motion to Amend "is debatable whenever the motion to which it is applied is debatable" (133, 397).

What is meant by a *friendly amendment*?

The term "friendly amendment" is described but once in *Robert's* (162), and then only with regard to a proposed change that the maker thinks will be seen as acceptable (or "friendly") to the maker of the original motion. Since a motion, once stated, belongs to the assembly, a "friendly amendment" must either be accepted by the body through unanimous consent or moved as an amendment. (See "Modify or Withdraw a Motion," page 97.)

If a friendly amendment is offered and accepted before the chair states the motion, may the person who seconded the motion withdraw his or her second?

Yes, but the chair does not again ask for a second because the person who suggested the modification (friendly amendment) has in effect seconded the motion (40–41).

What confusion occasionally occurs when an amendment to the constitution or bylaws is proposed?

A member may forget that a proposed amendment to the constitution or bylaws—or anything already adopted—is a main motion, not an amendment, and is therefore open to primary and secondary amendments. (See "Bylaws," pages 139–40.)

What is meant by "amendments must fall within the scope of previous notice"?

Robert's states that previous notice means "that notice of the proposal to be brought up . . . must be announced at the preceding meeting or must be included in the 'call' of the meeting at which it is to be considered" (4), and should be applied to motions "that have the effect of changing or nullifying previous action of the assembly" (122). With respect to amendments to bylaws—the most likely application of the question—*Robert's* states that the purpose of previous notice is "to alert the members to the proposed amendment so that all those interested can arrange to be present at its consideration" (581).

The relationship between notice and the amending process, then, is that any amendment to a motion that requires notice is in order only if the amendment is within the scope of notice. Without this restriction, the amending process could be used to defeat the purpose of requiring notice. For example, if the bylaws state that dues are $100 and notice is given of intent to amend by striking $100 and inserting $110, an amendment to strike $110 and insert any amount between $100 and $110 would be in order; but an amendment to strike $110 and insert an amount greater than $110 would be out of order. Again, the point is that members were notified that the dues might increase by as much as $10. There was no notice (warning) that the dues might be increased by more than $10. (See "Bylaws," pages 138–41.)

Is the expression "can amend down but not up" the same as "amendments must fall within the scope of notice"?

No. Although this expression is sometimes used, it is only half correct. An amendment cannot be higher (greater) than notice; but an amendment cannot be lower than the notice, either. Thus, in the example above, any amendment to strike $110 and insert an amount lower than $100 would be out of order. Notice was not given that the dues might be lowered. Thus, the phrase "can amend down but not up" should be replaced with "amendments must fall within the scope of notice."

Previous notice provides protection for the absent member, and amendments must fall within the scope of previous notice so that the amending process cannot be used to circumvent this protection.

Substitute

What is the difference between the motion to Amend and the motion to substitute?

Procedurally, they are practically the same (which makes sense, as the motion to substitute is a type of amendment). The difference is in the scope of the proposed change. *Robert's* says, "A motion to *Amend* by striking out an entire paragraph, section, or article—or a complete main motion or resolution—and inserting a different paragraph or other unit in its place is called a motion to *substitute*, and the paragraph or resolution to be inserted is said to be offered (or proposed as a 'substitute')" (153). For *Robert's*, once an amendment becomes as long as a paragraph, it becomes a motion to substitute. In practice, if one wishes to make a single change in a motion, one moves to amend the motion; if one wishes to make many changes at a time, one moves to substitute.

Is the motion to substitute handled in the same way as the motion to Amend?

Procedurally, the motion to substitute is handled like the motion to Amend. *Robert's* does provide one difference called the *perfecting process*, but it is seldom used. (See "Perfecting Process," pages 30–31.)

Since the motion to substitute is in effect a primary amendment, can one have a motion to substitute for the motion to substitute?

Yes, *Robert's* states in a footnote (with small print), "It is thus possible to introduce a proposed 'substitute for a substitute,' which cannot be amended, since it is a secondary amendment" (154), but offers little encouragement for using the secondary (second-degree) motion to substitute. If members are not familiar with parliamentary procedure, it would be better to withhold the secondary motion to substitute until the vote has been taken on the motion to substitute. The secondary (now simply the second) motion to substitute can then take on the winner (but see *Robert's* 161–62 for possible limitations).

When a motion to substitute is pending, can debate go into the merits of the original motion?

Yes, "debate may go fully into the merits of both the original text and the substitute" (154). If a member prefers the motion to substitute, she can address the weakness in the main motion; it is also germane for the opponent of the motion to substitute to point out the strengths of the main motion. (Compare to "Postpone Indefinitely," page 21, and "Reconsider," page 105.)

What confusion often results when the motion to substitute is used?

When the vote is taken on the motion to substitute, the question is which motion (the pending main motion or the motion to substitute) is now the main motion? The confusion arises when some members mistakenly assume that, if the motion to substitute passes, the assembly has adopted the substitute motion. Actually, the assembly has decided only to consider a modified main motion. In other words, the amending process is an editing process.

The chair can help prevent confusion in two ways. First, the chair should state "The question is: shall the motion to substitute replace the main motion as the main motion before the assembly?" or, "Shall the Johnson motion replace the Smith motion as the main motion before the assembly?"

If a large assembly is facing a complicated and controversial question, such as the adoption of the budget, one might even use different colors of paper. For example, the budget has been distributed on white paper, and a group decides to present a substitute budget. Tell them to run off copies on green paper. Then when the motion to substitute is presented, the chair says, "The question is: shall the green-paper budget replace the white-paper budget as the main motion before the assembly?" If the delegates still do not understand, the chair can add, "An 'Aye' vote means you want the green-paper budget to become the main motion before the assembly. A 'No' vote means you want to keep the white-paper budget as the main motion before the assembly."

Don't laugh—after three days at a convention, with the budget the last and most heated item of business and long days and late evenings taking their toll, delegates will appreciate all the help they can get. Finally, if there are three proposed budgets, have the third budget printed on blue paper. The chair should then say, "There are three budgets before the assembly. The first question is: shall the blue-paper budget replace the green-paper budget as the motion to substitute?"

Second, when the motion to substitute is pending, the chair should refer to it precisely as such: the motion to substitute. If the motion to substitute is adopted, then refer to it as the *substitute main motion* or *the main motion as amended.*

The Perfecting Process (Used with the Motion to Substitute)

What is meant by "the perfecting process"?

The perfecting process is the one difference in procedure between the motion to Amend and the motion to substitute. *Robert's* says that "when a motion to *substitute* is under consideration the paragraph [or section or article] to be struck out as well as the paragraph [or section or article] to be inserted can be perfected by secondary amendment" (154). *Robert's* provides the rationale:

> The rules for the treatment of motions to *substitute* automatically operate in fairness to both sides when there is disagreement as to the preferability of the original or the substitute. Under the procedure of initially accepting amendments to each element of the primary amendment exclusively—which is generally indicated whenever such disagreement exists—the proponents of the original version are first given the opportunity to amend their proposition into a more acceptable form in the light of conditions revealed by the introduction of the substitute. When this process is correctly handled . . . it tends to ensure that the provisions of the version first offered receive appropriate consideration, without impeding free debate of the proposal to substitute. By the requirement that internal amendment of the substitute be done before the vote on the motion to make the substitution, the members are protected from having to decide whether to reject the original version without knowing what may finally replace it. (157–58)

Hardcastle explains that the perfecting process is based on "the principle that each member who offers an original main motion has the right to have his motion considered by the assembly in the form in which it was presented and members have the right to perfect it by amendments, if desired."[29] The rationale, then, is fair play. If you allow only the motion to substitute to be susceptible to secondary amendments, you are giving proponents of the motion to substitute the advantage of perfecting their proposal while at the same time keeping the main motion in its original (less attractive) form.

Why is the perfecting process seldom, if ever, used?

In theory, the rationale for the perfecting process makes sense: it's not much fun to argue against fair play. But the case for the perfecting process is much ado about very little. Most of the time, the assembly simply argues about and votes on the motion to substitute. Then the motion that survives the first vote is open to any final perfecting. (*Robert's* does have limitations on what can be done to a substitute once adopted, which few organizations follow or realize exist.) Or, if the assembly does choose to amend the motion to substitute, it is usually for the purpose of compromise—of getting the motion closer to the main motion. The result is that everyone's views will have been considered and the will of the majority is served.[30]

Organizations occasionally exclude the perfecting process by adopting a special rule: the motion to substitute shall be treated as a motion to Amend. Most organizations simply ignore the perfecting process. Seldom do we see the device strictly followed. However, we have seen the perfecting process solve complicated problems during a convention. It did take careful explanation twice by the chair—once two hours before it was to be used and again at the time of its use. (This procedurally sophisticated group also made liberal use of Objection to the Consideration of a Question, Postpone Indefinitely, and the qualified call for the Previous Question.)

Create a Blank

What is meant by "creating and filling a blank"?

Although the motion to create a blank is an incidental motion, *Robert's* discusses the motion in the section on amendments because the motion is, in effect, a third-degree amendment. "Filling blanks, although not a form of amendment in itself, is a closely related device by which an unlimited number of alternative choices for a particular specification in a main motion or primary amendment can be pending at the same time" (162).[31] When, for example, an assembly cannot reach agreement on dues or a date for a future convention, creating a blank is a seldom used and little understood but valuable procedure.

What is the procedure for creating and filling a blank?

Robert's provides three ways to create a blank and three ways to fill a blank. To create a blank,

1. a member moves a motion or an amendment containing a blank,
2. a member moves to create a blank, or
3. the chair requests unanimous consent to create a blank (163–64).

A blank can be filled with names, amounts of money, or places, dates, or numbers (164–66).

The procedure for filling a blank varies slightly depending on whether the blank is to be filled with a name, an amount of money, a place, a date, or a number. Using a motion to set the dues as an example, the procedure to create and fill a blank is as follows:

1. A member moves to strike the amount and create a blank. The motion requires a second, but it is neither debatable nor amendable. If it is obvious to the chair that the situation calls for creating a blank, the chair may suggest that a blank be created: "If there is no objection, we will create a blank."

2. After the blank is created, the chair states, "Are there suggestions for filling the blank?" Without requiring a second, each member can suggest one amount to fill it. (The amount struck to create the blank automatically becomes one of the proposals for filling it.)

3. Debate is open on all the suggestions, so long as the motion is debatable. *Robert's* states, "Each proposal is treated as an independent original to be voted on separately until one is approved by a majority" (164). Interpreted literally, this statement would mean that each suggestion is debated separately, which makes little sense. Debate in favor of one suggestion is debate against the other suggestions; thus, debate is open on all suggestions at once.[32]

4. The vote is taken on which suggestion will fill the blank, beginning with the least popular choice. The chair should explain to the members the importance of voting "No" as well as "Aye." If members wait to vote "Aye" on their choice but neglect to vote "No" on the early suggestions, one of those suggestions may be adopted and the blank filled.

5. As soon as a suggestion receives a majority vote, the chair states that the blank has been filled and debate is open on the main motion.

Why is filling a blank seldom used?

In most cases, a secondary amendment is sufficient. Also, because the device is somewhat complicated, care must be taken when creating and filling a blank. However, since dues and budgets are often controversial issues, creating and filling a blank is an excellent way to ensure that minority views will be heard and that a majority view will emerge.[33]

Commit or Refer

How may the motion to Refer be made?

The motion to Refer may be made in either the unqualified or the qualified form:

1. In the unqualified form, the proposer states, "I move to refer the main motion to the [such and such] committee."

2. In the qualified form, the proposer adds one or more of the following: names of the committee members, instructions for the committee, dates when the committee should report (171–72). "I move to refer the main motion to a committee consisting of Ms. X, Mr. Y, and Ms. Z, with instructions to interview each department supervisor and report at the June meeting."

What are the different kinds of committees?

There are two kinds of ordinary committees:

1. Standing, which are established in the bylaws (or by a special rule) and have a continuing existence. A standing committee is a permanent committee (490–91).

2. Special (or ad hoc), which are created for a specific task and cease to exist as soon as that committee's task is completed (492). Completed means "on presentation of its final report to the assembly" (492). A special committee is a temporary committee.

A committee may be given one of three general tasks: *investigation* (all factions represented, neutral chair); *action* (members who supported proposal for action); or *editing* (clearinghouse for motions to be considered at a convention).

May an amendment be referred?

Not alone, but such a motion can be made to the main motion while an amendment is pending. If adopted, the amendment follows the main motion (132). Some convention rules permit an amendment to be referred to committee, so that the main motion can remain and be acted upon.

Committees

Is it a good idea for a committee to have co-chairs?

No. "The anomalous title 'co-chairman' should be avoided, as it causes impossible dilemmas in attempts to share the functions of a single position" (176). If the committee's task is heavy, appoint a vice-chair.

If a main motion is referred to committee, what happens to any motions that were pending at the time the main motion was referred?

Pending amendments accompany the main motion to committee. A pending motion to Postpone Indefinitely is dropped (128, 177, 519). Although *Robert's* gives complete details about how the main motion and pending amendments are handled (503–29), generally the assembly can consider the motion to Refer a very flexible motion, and the committee has great latitude in dealing with the subject matter contained in the main motion.

> FREEDOM OF ACTION AFTER REFERRAL. Once a committee to which a resolution or other main motion has been referred commences its deliberations, the committee is free to consider, and recommend for adoption, any amendment to the resolution or motion so referred, without regard to whether or not the assembly, prior to the referral, considered the same or a similar amendment and either adopted or rejected it. (176)

In other words, the committee's task is to search, find the best answer, and report it to the assembly.

What rules of procedure should a committee use?

The procedure in a committee (commonly a small number of persons) is much less formal and mirrors the relaxed procedures for smaller boards outlined on pages 487–88 of *Robert's*:

1. Members speak informally. "Members may raise a hand instead of standing when seeking to obtain the floor, and may remain seated while making motions or speaking" (487).

2. Discussion of a subject is permitted while no motion is pending.

3. The chair may take an active part in the discussion and may also make motions. "In committees, the chairman is usually the most active participant in the discussions and work of the committee" (500).

4. Motions do not require a second.

5. There is no limit to the number of times a member may speak to a subject or motion.

6. Motions to limit or close debate (Previous Question) are out of order (191, 198, 500).

7. When consensus is clear to all members, decisions may be made without either a formal motion or a vote.

8. "During actual deliberations of the committee, only committee members have the right to be present" (501). Although committee deliberations are closed, "When a committee is to make substantive recommendations or decisions on an important matter, it should give members of the society an opportunity to appear before it and present their views on the subject" (501).

9. A motion to Reconsider a vote can be made and taken up regardless of the time elapsed since the vote was taken (329). There is no limit to the number of times a question can be reconsidered. The motion to Reconsider may be made by any member of the committee who did not vote with the losing side, including members who abstained or were absent. Also, "Unless all the members of the committee who voted with the prevailing side are present or have been notified that the reconsideration will be moved, it requires a *two-thirds vote* to adopt the motion to *Reconsider*" (330).

10. A committee may appoint subcommittees, which are responsible to the committee. Unless the organization provides otherwise, subcommittee members must be chosen from the members of the committee (497).

Robert's states that large committees (more than about twelve members present) generally follow more formal procedures (9–10, 501). However, since a committee cannot adopt its own rules, the 11th Edition notes: "If a standing or special committee is so large that it can function best in the manner of a full-scale assembly, it should be instructed that the informalities and modifications of the regular rules of parliamentary procedure listed for small boards on pages 487–88 are not to apply to its proceedings" (501).

What are the rights of the president who is an ex officio member of a committee?

Ex officio is commonly misunderstood to mean "a member without the right to vote." The term correctly means "by virtue of the office," and the president, being a member of the committee by virtue of office, has the same full rights granted any member of the committee. The only differences are that the president does not have an obligation to participate and is not counted in the quorum (456–57, 497).

What are the rights of an ex officio member of a committee?

If a person is a member of the organization, there is no distinction between ex officio and regular membership. An ex officio committee member who is not a member of the organization has all of the privileges but none of the obligations of membership and is not counted in determining a quorum (483–84, 497).

Is a committee required to keep a record of its proceedings?

No, *Robert's* takes a casual approach to recording minutes, stating that only "a brief memorandum in the nature of minutes for the use of the committee" is required (500). Given the nature of the committee and concerns today for open meetings and accountability, a more formal approach may be warranted.

What if the committee chair fails or refuses to call a meeting of the committee?

If the chair fails to call a meeting, "the committee must meet on the call of any two of its members," unless the governing documents provide otherwise (499).

May the chair of a committee replace an uncooperative member?

No, not unless the committee chair appointed the member (177, 497). Only the body that created the committee has the authority to change the membership of the committee. The chair may, of course, request that the offending member be removed as a committee member. In most organizations, the president appoints committee members and is therefore the person who can remove them.

May a committee discipline an uncooperative member?

A committee cannot impose a penalty on a disruptive member, but can only report such behavior to a parent body for action (501). However, the 11th Edition gives greater authority to committees to control their proceedings. In the event a committee member disrupts a meeting and there is no opportunity for the parent body "within the time needed to effectively resolve the problem and enable the committee to complete its assigned tasks," the committee may require "the disorderly member to leave the meeting room during the remainder of the meeting" (501). The 11th Edition also makes clear that the procedures outlined in "Dealing with Offenses in a Meeting" apply to committee meetings (501, 645–49).

How should a committee organize its report?

The committee report should consist of two parts:

1. the report, which consists of background information, such as the charge of the committee, how it carried out its charge, and the possible solutions it considered (503–10, 511–14), and
2. the recommendation, which is the proposal for action based on the background information (504–5).

The first part is sometimes referred to as the *body*, but it is common practice to refer to both parts as the *report*. The important point is not what the parts are called but the distinction between them.

May a committee report be amended by the assembly?

Generally, a committee report may not be amended on the principle that the assembly has no right to make a committee say something it does not want to say.[34] This principle does not pose a problem. The committee should distinguish between its report (background information) and its recommendation (proposal for action). The report may not be amended, but the recommendation is a main motion, subject to the rules and procedures of a main motion, and may be amended.

When a committee reports, what does the assembly do after it receives the report?

Nothing; it simply listens to the report as it would in the case of a progress or annual report. After the chair of the committee completes the report, the chair of the assembly states, "You have heard [read] the report of the _____ committee. Are there any questions? [*Pause*] There being no [further] questions, that completes the report of the _____ committee." The chair does *not* ask for a motion to receive, to approve, or to accept the committee report. No action is required.

It is such a common error to "receive" or "approve" or "accept" committee reports that it is wise to refer extensively to *Robert's*:

> It should be noted that a motion "to receive" a communication after it has been read is meaningless and should therefore be avoided. (28)
>
> A common error is to move that a report "be received" after it has been read—apparently on the supposition that such a motion is necessary in order for the report to be taken under consideration or to be recorded as having been made. In fact, this motion is meaningless, since the report has already been received. Even before a report has been read, a motion to receive it is unnecessary if the time for its reception is established by the order of business, or if no member objects.
>
> Another error—less common, but dangerous—is to move, after the report has been read (or even before the reading), that it "be accepted," when the actual intent is that of the mistaken motion to receive, as just explained, or of a legitimate motion to receive made *before* the report is read. If a motion "to accept" made under any of these circumstances is adopted and is given its proper interpretation, it implies that the assembly has endorsed the complete report. (508)

Although the advice in *Robert's* is well taken, it is disappointing that the authors did not end the confusion over *approve, accept, agree to,* and *adopt* by throwing out all terms except *adopt* (124–25, 508). *Robert's* admits the confusion exists: "As applied to an assembly's action with respect to board or committee reports or any of their contents, the expressions *adopt, accept,* and *agree to* are all equivalent—that is, the text adopted becomes in effect the act or statement of the assembly. It is usually best to use the word *adopt*, however, since it is the least likely to be misunderstood" (508).

The custom of many organizations is to move to accept all committee reports, and custom dies hard. However, this custom can be dangerous. Suppose following the announcement of ballot election results, the committee asks that the elections report be "adopted." Could the body, by amending or rejecting the committee's report, alter the outcome of the election? The point is simple: if no action is proposed by the committee, just listen to (or read) the report, and ask any questions. Then move on to the next item of business.

Bottom line: Avoid use of the terms *receive, approve, accept, agree to.* Keep it simple, clear, and easy to understand. So, for a committee report, do nothing; for a committee recommendation, move to adopt.

When a committee report includes recommendations, how are the recommendations dealt with?

The word *recommendation* has two meanings:

1. A committee recommendation is usually a proposal for action, and the proper motion is to move to adopt the recommendation. At this point, the recommendation becomes a main motion and is treated like any other main motion before the assembly. Recommendation, then, simply means main motion.

2. When a committee functions as a clearinghouse for motions, such as a resolutions or bylaws committee for conventions, the word recommendation acquires a different meaning. Organizations often require that proposed amendments to the bylaws, resolutions, and new business items be submitted to a committee for the purpose of rewriting, editing, and combining with other motions of the same subject matter. When the committee reports to the assembly, each of the motions sent to the committee becomes pending automatically, with no motion being made by the committee. If the committee wishes, or is charged, to state the committee's opinion on the pending motion, the chair of the committee states, "Resolution three is before the assembly, and the committee recommends its adoption." In this context, the recommendation of the committee is not a main motion; rather, it is the committee's opinion—its advice—to the assembly on

how to vote on the motion that was sent to and considered by the committee. Recommendation in this case means advice (633–36).

Too often, inexperienced committee chairs fail to distinguish between the two meanings of recommendation, and the result is utter confusion. The chair of a resolutions committee, for example, moves that resolution six be adopted. (Although *Robert's* says the resolutions are automatically pending and no motion is required, by custom most committee chairs move the motions.) Then, since the committee does not approve of a later resolution, the chair says, "The committee moves that the resolution not be adopted." Such a mess. Now the delegates vote "Aye" if they are against the motion and "No" if they are for the resolution! The chair has neglected to keep the main motion, which must always be moved in the affirmative, separate from the committee's opinion of the main motion (517–18).

The chair should state, "Resolution five is before the assembly, and the committee recommends that you vote in favor of the resolution. . . . [After vote] Resolution six is before the assembly, and the committee recommends that you vote against the resolution." (See "Resolution," pages 18–19, for committee procedure for reviewing continuing resolutions.) Regardless of the recommendation of the committee, votes are for or against the resolution (and not the recommendation of the committee). That is, "Those in favor of Resolution six, say 'Aye.' Those opposed, say 'No.'"

What if committee members cannot agree on a report or recommendation?

The minority within the committee can prepare a minority report. Unlike Robert in his 1915 *Rules of Order Revised*, *Robert's* refers to the "'so-called' minority report" (527) to signal that a minority report "is a privilege that the assembly may accord, not a matter of right" (528).[35]

The procedure for presenting a minority report is as follows:

1. Inform the chair of the assembly that the minority would like to present a separate report to the assembly.

2. After the chair of the committee presents the committee report and moves to adopt the report, the chair of the assembly calls on a committee member for the minority report. The presentation

of a minority report is a privilege, not a right (528). Thus, the chair should call for the minority report unless someone objects. If there is objection, a majority vote without debate is required to consider a minority report (528–29). In this instance, it is a distinction without a difference. If the assembly refuses to consider the minority report, any member may move to substitute the recommendations of the minority for those recommended by the committee (529).

3. A member of the committee presents the minority report and moves to substitute the minority report for the majority report. At this point, the assembly has a main motion (committee report) and a primary amendment (minority view) on the floor.

4. Technically, debate is open on the primary amendment (to substitute). In effect, debate is on which report will be the main motion before the assembly. "The question is: shall the minority report replace the committee report as the main motion before the assembly?" When the assembly votes, the first vote does not adopt either report. The first vote decides which report will be considered by the organization as its pending main motion. It is important to remember that the motion to substitute the minority report is treated like any other motion to substitute.

Do committee recommendations require a second?

No. Since the recommendation is the desire of more than one member, the rationale requiring a second has been met (36, 80, 119–20). No additional second is needed from the floor.

Do motions need to be seconded within smaller boards or committees?

No. Smaller boards and committees operate under more relaxed rules. Motions do not need to be seconded in a board meeting where there are not more than about a dozen members present (488). The same informalities apply to all but the largest committees (501).

What is a reference committee?

Some parliamentary authorities, including *The Standard Code,* use reference committees to hold hearings on resolutions assigned to them and to recommend a course of action on each proposal.

Committee of the Whole, Quasi Committee of the Whole, Informal Consideration

What are the purposes of the committee of the whole, quasi committee of the whole, and informal consideration?

Each is a variation of the motion to Refer. The object "is not to turn the main question over to a smaller group, but to permit the assembly's full meeting body to consider it with the greater freedom of debate that is allowed in committees—that is, with no limit on the number of times a member can speak" (168, 533–34). Greater freedom of debate does not mean that committee informality is observed.

Device	Size of Meeting	Role of Chair	Results of Votes Taken
Committee of the whole	Large	New chair	Votes not final
Quasi committee of the whole	Medium	Chair remains	Votes not final
Informal consideration	Small	Chair remains	Votes final

What are the differences between committee of the whole, quasi committee of the whole, and informal consideration?

As the table shows, there are three "essential distinctions," dealing with the size of the meeting, the role of the presiding officer, and the results of the votes taken (530–31).[36] Additional differences are discussed in *Robert's* 531–41, but these are among the last pages you will ever need or want to read.

Are motions to go into and get out of committee of the whole debatable?

The motion to go into a committee of the whole is debatable (531–32, 538), but the motion to rise and report is not debatable (533–34).

How does an assembly get into and out of the committee of the whole?

The following steps are taken:

1. A member states, "I move to go into a committee of the whole," or, "I move that the assembly resolve itself into a committee of the whole to . . ."

2. If the motion is adopted, the presiding officer calls upon another member to become chair of the committee of the whole and takes a place as a member of the assembly.

3. When discussion in the committee of the whole is completed, a member moves "to rise and report."

4. If the motion is adopted, the presiding officer of the assembly returns to the chair and calls on the chair of the committee of the whole for a committee report.

This procedure seems silly becau se it is silly. All three of these variations of the motion to Refer should be left unused. If restrictions on debate seem to be a problem, members can simply move to suspend the rules regarding the restrictions (e.g., number of speeches).[37] (See "Suspend the Rules," pages 76–79.)

Postpone to a Certain Time (or Definitely)

Is the motion to Postpone to a Certain Time the same as the motion to Postpone Definitely?

Yes. The Motion to Postpone to a Certain Time is also referred to as "Postpone Definitely," or simply as "Postpone."

When should the motion to Postpone to a Certain Time be used?

A main motion "may be postponed either so that it may be considered at a more convenient time, or because debate has shown reasons for holding off a decision until later" (180). The motion may be postponed to later in the same meeting (either to a specific time or to a point prior to or following a specific business item or event) or to the following meeting (where it will become unfinished business unless it was postponed to a specific time or to a point before or after a certain business item or event) so long as the organization meets at least quarterly.

May debate on the motion to Postpone to a Certain Time go into the merits of the main motion?

No. "[Debate] must not go into the merits of the main question any more than is necessary to enable the assembly to decide whether the main question should be postponed and to what time" (182).

How long may a main motion be postponed?

If an organization meets less often than at quarterly intervals, a main motion may be postponed only to the end of the same session; if an organization meets at least within quarterly intervals, a main motion may be postponed to the end of the next session (183, 364). In other words, for organizations with regular business meetings, a main motion may be postponed to the end of the following meeting. But at an annual convention, the assembly cannot postpone a main motion (resolution, new business item) to the next convention (87, 90–91, 183).

Because no new main motion with the same subject matter may be made while a motion is postponed and because motions postponed for a long period of time tend to complicate procedure, it is wise to follow the limitation.

When a main motion is postponed, what happens to any pending amendments?

When a motion is postponed, any pending motions (Postpone Indefinitely, Amend, Refer) are postponed with the main motion. When consideration of the postponed main motion is resumed, the business is in the same condition as it was when the motion was postponed. For example, a main motion with a motion to Amend and a motion to Refer is postponed until unfinished business. When the assembly reaches unfinished business, the chair states, "We turn now to the motion to . . . which was postponed until unfinished business. Also pending is a motion to Amend by . . . and a motion to Refer. Debate is now open on the motion to Refer."

What confusion results between the motion to Postpone to a Certain Time and the motion to Lay on the Table?

Members usually misuse the motion to Lay on the Table when they mean to Postpone to a Certain Time. There is no such motion as "to lay on the table until 4:00 P.M." or "to table until the next meeting." (See "Lay on the Table," pages 60–62.) The motion to Postpone to a Certain Time is a motion that should be used more often. For example:

If you want to postpone discussion of the dues until after the budget is adopted, say, "I move to postpone consideration of the dues until after action is taken on the budget."

If you want to postpone consideration of an item until missing members arrive in the afternoon, say, "I move to postpone until 3:00 P.M."

If you believe an item needs additional study, say, "I move to postpone until the next meeting."

May a class of business or several items be postponed?

No (184–85). The same answer applies to the motion to Lay on the Table (211).

May an amendment be postponed?

Not alone, but such a motion can be made to the main motion while an amendment is pending. If adopted, the amendment follows the main motion (132).

Creating Orders

What is meant by an "order"?

A question (main motion) that has been postponed becomes an order to consider the motion at a later time. This order is called an *order of the day*. In other words, when members adopt a motion to Postpone, they are ordering the organization (themselves) to consider the question at a later time (185–88, 352, 364–65).

Orders of the day are divided into classes of *general* orders and *special* orders (186, 352, 364).

What is the difference between a general order and a special order?

A general order requires a majority vote and does not interrupt business when the time to which it was postponed arrives. A special order requires a two-thirds vote and interrupts business when the time to which it was postponed arrives.

How does a general or a special order relate to the motion to Postpone to a Certain Time?

The motion to Postpone to a Certain Time in effect creates an order for the assembly to consider a main motion later.

What is the form for creating orders with the motion to Postpone to a Certain Time?

A general order takes this form: "I move to postpone the main motion until 4:00 this afternoon." The motion requires a majority vote and will not interrupt pending business at 4:00 P.M. This is the form for a special order: "I move to postpone the main motion until 4:00 this afternoon and make it a special order." The motion requires a two-thirds vote and will interrupt business pending at 4:00 P.M.

Any motion to Postpone that is adopted without being made a special order is a general order (186, 365).

Is the motion to Postpone to a Certain Time the only way to create an order?

No. Although creating orders relates primarily to the motion to Postpone, *Robert's* lists two other ways to create an order:

1. by the adoption of a main motion to consider at a future time an item that is not yet before the assembly, or
2. by the adoption of an agenda or program. (365)

Does a special order always interrupt business when the time to which it was postponed arrives?

No. A special order interrupts nearly all matters of business, but it neither interrupts nor takes precedence over motions to Recess or Adjourn. Although unlikely to occur, a special order also does not interrupt questions of privilege, special orders that were made before this special order was made, or *the* special order for a meeting (187, 369).

If more than one general or special order has been created for the same hour, or if postponed motions come into conflict with one another, in what order are the postponed motions taken up?

If several orders were made for the same time, they are taken up in the order in which they were made. The question of taking up several postponed motions can be complicated (see 367–71.) The good news is that it is highly unlikely to happen.

What should a member do if the chair forgets that a general or special order is due?

If a member adheres to traditional parliamentary procedure, the proper device is to Call for the Orders of the Day. Since the device is archaic, the member should rise to a Parliamentary Inquiry or to a Point of Order.

Call for the Orders of the Day

What is the purpose of calling for the orders of the day?

A Call for the Orders of the Day is a demand that the agenda be followed or that a general or special order be considered (219).

Does the member include the reason for calling for the orders of the day?

No. "The call must be simply 'for the orders of the day' and not for a specified one, as this motion is only a demand that the proper schedule of business—whatever it is—be followed" (220).

What should the chair do if a member calls for the orders of the day but the assembly prefers to complete the pending business?

In a convention, consideration of an item often extends beyond the time limit established in the agenda. When the chair senses that the assembly prefers to complete the item rather than adhere to the agenda, the chair may do one of two things:

1. The chair states, "The orders of the day are called for. The orders of the day are . . . The question is: Will the assembly proceed to the orders of the day?" (223). If two-thirds vote in the negative, the assembly continues to consider the pending item and does not turn to the item listed in the agenda.

2. Since the item pending is no doubt foremost in the minds of the assembly, it may be clearer to present the question on whether the assembly wishes to continue consideration of the item. The chair states, "The orders of the day are called for. The orders of the day are . . . To continue consideration of the pending item requires a two-thirds vote to suspend the rules. The question is: Shall the rules be suspended to continue consideration of the pending business?"

As stated earlier, the motion to Call for the Orders of the Day is archaic, and many parliamentary authorities, such as Keesey, *The Standard Code*, and Lochrie have retired "this quaint phrase."[38] If a member notices that the chair has forgotten that it is time to consider an item on the agenda, the member may remind the chair through a Parliamentary Inquiry or a Point of Order.

Limit or Extend Limits of Debate

How many ways may a member move to limit or extend limits of debate?

Debate is limited or extended according to the number of speakers (preferably on each side), the length of each speech, or the total time allowed for debate (191).

Does the motion to Limit or Extend Limits of Debate apply to all pending motions?

With respect to pending motions, the motion to Limit or Extend Limits of Debate can be made in either of two ways:

1. the unqualified form—"I move to limit debate to five more minutes"—which applies only to the immediately pending motion, or
2. the qualified form—"I move to limit debate on the amendment and on the main motion to a total of twenty minutes"—which can apply to all pending motions.

Robert's states that a motion to Limit or Extend Limits of Debate can be "applied to any immediately pending debatable motion, to an entire series of pending debatable motions, or to any consecutive part of such a series beginning with the immediately pending question" (192). (See "Previous Question (Close Debate)," pages 55–57, for the same procedure and for examples of how the qualified form works.)

Is the motion to Limit or Extend Limits of Debate debatable?

Yes and no, usually no.

Yes, the motion to Limit or Extend Limits of Debate is debatable if it is made when no main motion is pending. The motion is then a main motion and open to debate.

No, the motion to Limit or Extend Limits of Debate is not debatable if it is moved when a main motion is on the floor. One way to determine whether a motion is debatable is to apply the following guideline: *a motion is debatable if debate does not defeat the purpose of the motion.* In this case, the purpose of the motion is to limit debate on the pending motion(s); to allow debate would defeat the purpose of the motion. If the motion were to extend the limits of debate, debate on the motion would be in conflict with the limitation on debate that is presently in force.

In those instances when the motion to Limit or Extend Limits of Debate is not debatable, how does a member obtain the floor to move to amend the motion?

If not recognized, the member should rise to a Point of Order or to a Parliamentary Inquiry to inform the chair of the wish to amend the motion.

Does limitation or extension of debate carry over to the following meeting?

No (195–96).

Does Limit or Extend Limits of Debate apply to motions that might be made while the order is in effect?

If a motion to limit debate is adopted, it applies to any debatable subsidiary motions, motions to Reconsider, and debatable appeals that may be made subsequently while the order is in force. An adopted motion to extend debate, however, affects only the motions that were pending when the order was adopted (193–94).

Without an adopted motion to limit debate, is there any time limit on a member's right to speak?

Yes, each member has the right to speak twice on the same question on the same day for no longer than ten minutes at a time (43, 387–88). Many members are not aware of, or ignore, this limitation. It is a great rule to know because it is the solution to the ever-present problem of what to do with the member who speaks several times on every question. (See "Postpone Indefinitely," pages 20–21.)

Paul Mason provides an interesting history to the ten-minute speaking limit:

> Here is a story, possibly authentic, which will illustrate the origin of Mr. Robert's rule that speeches are limited to ten minutes. An elderly person in New York City claims to have taken Mr. Robert over to a meeting of a tennis club on Long Island.

That club had the rule that speeches could not be longer than ten minutes and Mr. Robert was reported to have been so impressed by the rule that he exclaimed, "By jove, I'll put that in my book."[39]

May a motion be referred or postponed after debate has been limited?

Robert's provides that a motion to Refer or Postpone cannot be moved after the adoption of a motion to close debate at a specific time or to limit total debate (170, 181–82). The premise behind this rule is that a motion to Refer or to Postpone conflicts with the order limiting debate. However, the premise is faulty, and this esoteric rule is rarely followed.

Is the motion to limit debate the best way for members to control what they believe to be excessive debate?

No. No motion begins with better intentions and ends by causing such a mess, particularly in conventions, than the motion to limit debate. The motion seems to have a sensible purpose—to promote efficiency in general and to muzzle loudmouths in particular. More often than not, however, the motion wastes rather than saves time; can create an unfair and confusing situation; and, at conventions where a card or flag system is used for recognition, exacerbates abuse of requests for information. Members who are weary of debate would be better served by more active use of the motion to close debate.[40]

Previous Question (Close Debate)

Why does *Robert's* use the phrase "Previous Question"?

Good question. Tradition, some would say; others would say that the authors are just being stubborn. "A term of art," says one author of the 1970 *Newly Revised*.[41] Whatever the reason, parliamentarians who wish to modernize procedure are in near agreement in their efforts to retire the phrase "call for the Previous Question."[42] In recent editions the authors have relented a bit and state, "A motion such as 'I call for [or 'call'] the question' or 'I move we vote now' is simply a motion for the *Previous Question* made in nonstandard form" (202). Given that the 11th Edition establishes "Request for Information" as the preferred name for the motion Point of Information, in an effort to reduce the common misunderstanding or misuse of this motion (xxvi), there is a compelling argument that it is past time to establish *close debate* as the preferred name for *previous question*. In fact, Robert sometimes used the form "the motion to close debate" in his writings (*Parliamentary Law*, 70).

The point is the chair should recognize and treat the nonstandard form as a motion to call the Previous Question. More, the clear, concise, accurate, sensible wording, "I move to close debate," should be considered standard. Doing so removes one of the examples of why people complain that parliamentary procedure seems to be written in code ("Calling for the Previous Question means to end debate on the present question?!"). But if you enjoy the more esoteric form, you should feel free to call for the Previous Question.

May a member move to close debate by calling out "Question"?

No. Many members mistakenly believe that a member can call (or scream) "Question!" without getting the floor and that this tactic constitutes a legitimate motion to close debate. Worse, some members believe such a call automatically ends debate. The point is that the motion to call for the Previous Question (to close debate) must be made in the same manner as most motions: the motion cannot interrupt the speaker, and the maker of the motion must be recognized by the chair before making the motion (207, 385).

Calling "Question" rather than waiting to be recognized is the result of *Robert's* tradition of having the chair bring debate to a close by asking, "Are you ready for the question?" to which members often reply, "Question," if ready for the vote. The 11th Edition addresses this confusion by adding, "Is there any further debate?" (44), a change recommended in previous editions of *Notes and Comments*.

Because members confuse this procedure with the formal motion to close debate and because this archaic exchange takes time, the chair should replace the traditional form, "Are you ready for the question?" with, "If there is no further debate, we will now vote." The chair should pause for a few seconds to honor the right of a member who wishes to rise to debate. Remember, the responsibility of the chair is to expedite business and to protect the rights of each member. For all debatable motions, "If there is no further debate . . ." is the best form for accomplishing these ends. Another reason to change terminology from *the previous question* to *close debate* is that it eliminates the rude, arrogant, insensitive misuse of shouting "Question."

May a member move to close debate immediately after the maker speaks to the motion?

Yes, but a bad yes. In describing characteristics of subsidiary motions as a class, the 10th edition stated: "The time when they are in order extends from the moment the question on a motion to which they can be applied is stated by the chair" (62). Read literally, it means that the motion to close debate could even be made by the maker of a debatable motion to prevent any debate. Kindly put, that makes no sense. The 11th Edition is a bit more elastic, stating that subsidiary motions are in order "during the entire time that a motion to which they can be applied is pending" (65). Thus the authors leave the answer as a shaky yes, but the attempt to close debate before debate has begun is the kind of tactic that leads to charges of unfairness and railroading. The chair should rule that close debate means that there must be an opportunity for at least one speech by each side. Some conventions state in their rules that the motion to close debate is not in order prior to the opportunity for at least one speech on each side.

May a member conclude his or her debate by moving to close debate?

Yes (116, 378). "When assigned the floor, a member may use it for any proper purpose, or a combination of purposes; for example, although a member may have begun by debating a pending motion, he may conclude by moving any secondary motion, including the *Previous Question*" (378). However, few tactics anger an assembly more. To prevent needless friction, an organization should adopt a special rule: a member, while speaking on a motion, may not move to close debate, or, a member debating a pending motion may not conclude his or her remarks with an undebatable motion (or, by moving to close debate). In contrast, *The Standard Code* provides that "it is out of order for a member to debate the issue and end the remarks with a motion to close debate."[43]

May the motion to close debate be applied to more than one pending motion?

Yes. The motion to close debate can be made in either of two ways, just like the motion to Limit or Extend Limits of Debate:

1. the unqualified form "I move to close debate," which applies only to the immediately pending motion, or
2. the qualified form "I move to close debate on all pending motions," which applies to any or all pending motions as long as they are consecutive and include the immediately pending motion.

The unqualified form is more common—far more common.

What guidelines apply when a member moves to close debate in the qualified form?

As mentioned above, there are two requirements:

1. The motion must include the immediately pending motion.
2. The motion must apply to consecutive motions (198–99, 207–9).

An example may help. Four motions—a main motion, Amend, Amend the amendment, and Refer to committee—are pending. A motion to close debate on all pending motions is in order; a motion to close debate on the motions to Refer, Amend the amendment, and Amend is in order; a motion to close debate on the motions to Refer and Amend the amendment is in order. All three qualified motions to close debate include the immediately pending motion (Refer) and are applied consecutively.

A motion to close debate on the motions to Amend the amendment, Amend, and the main motion is out of order (because it does not include the immediately pending motion); a motion to close debate on the motions to Refer and to Amend and the main motion is out of order (because it does not apply to consecutive motions).

May an unqualified motion to close debate be changed to a qualified motion to close debate?

Yes. The qualified call for the Previous Question is a special characteristic that permits an effect similar to that of amendment. Before the vote is taken on a motion to close debate, a member may move to close debate in the qualified form. If several motions are pending, another member may move to close debate in yet another qualified form. In each case, the member must obtain the floor, and the motion requires a second.[44]

If two or more qualified motions to close debate are pending at the same time, in what order are they voted on?

The vote is taken first on the motion that would close debate on the largest number of motions; if this motion fails, vote on the one to close the next smaller number. Continue until one is adopted by a two-thirds vote or until all of the motions to close debate have been rejected (200). Again, an example may help. Four motions—main motion, Amend, Amend the amendment, and Refer—are pending. A member moves to close debate. A second member moves to close debate on all pending motions. A third member moves to close debate on the motions to Refer and to Amend the amendment. Three motions to close debate are on the floor. The motion to close debate on all pending motions is voted on first; if it is adopted, debate is closed, and the next vote is on the motion to Refer. If the motion to close debate on all pending motions fails, the next vote is on the motion to close debate on Refer and on the amendment to the amendment. If the motion fails, the third vote is on the unqualified motion to close debate.

You may wonder why so much attention has been devoted to the qualified motion to close debate, a motion with which few members and delegates are familiar. The reason is that it can be very helpful. If several motions—four, for example—are pending and you are tired of all the debate, one motion, "Close debate on all pending motions," is far more efficient than four separate motions to close debate. If a main motion, a motion to Amend, and a motion to Amend the amendment are pending and you have been waiting for the opportunity to amend the main motion, the motion to close debate on both the primary and secondary amendments is the most efficient motion to use.

What confusion often occurs when the assembly votes on a motion to close debate?

When a motion to close debate is put to the vote, members are often confused about what they are voting on. For example, if a main motion and a motion to close debate are pending and the chair says, "Those in favor of the motion, say 'Aye,'" it is easy to see why a member could become confused. What motion is being voted on? It is the responsibility of the chair, through one of two options, to eliminate any chance of confusion.

First, the chair should always include the name of the motion that is being voted on: "Those in favor of closing debate, say 'Aye.' Those opposed to closing debate, say 'No.'" (*Robert's* recommends a "rising vote" on 207–8, but that may be unnecessary when it is obvious that the motion to close debate will pass.) Simply replacing the words "the motion" with "closing debate" eliminates any chance of confusion. It's really not too much to ask of the chair.

Second, the chair can use the unanimous-consent shortcut: "If there is no objection, we will close debate and vote on the main motion." If the chair senses that members want to stop debate, the unanimous-consent shortcut has the advantage of expediting business (by not taking the vote on the motion to close debate and eliminating the possibility of confusion about what motion is being voted on) (54–56).

May the motion to close debate be applied to undebatable motions?

Yes, Previous Question may be applied to motions that are amendable, but not debatable (198–99, 231, 243, 271).

Robert's states that the application "seldom serves a useful purpose" (243), and Keesey says this "appears to be an unnecessarily complicated device" (52), which applies to the motions to Limit or Extend Limits of Debate, Recess, Division of a Question, and Fix the Time to Which to Adjourn and also to motions relating to methods of nominations and voting. Keesey is correct—few members, if any, will see the motion to close debate used for this purpose. Not even a trivia expert will find this information helpful.

May the chair close debate?

No (44, 386–87). The chair may, however, signal that most members appear to be ready to vote by switching from the question, "Is there further debate?" to the statement, "If there is no further debate, we will vote on . . ."

Lay on the Table

What is the purpose of the motion to Lay on the Table?

Lay on the Table permits an assembly to temporarily lay the pending question aside when "something else of immediate urgency has arisen" or "something else needs to be addressed before consideration of the pending question is resumed." (209). *Robert's* terminology, which is archaic, grew out of the legislative custom of laying a bill on the clerk's table to await further consideration. A more accurate form would be, as *The Standard Code*, 4th edition suggests, to *postpone temporarily.*[45]

When a main motion is laid on the table, do any pending motions accompany the main motion?

Yes, all pending motions accompany the main motion to the table.

How long may the main motion remain on the table before expiring?

In organizations meeting at least quarterly, the motion remains on the table until the end of the following meeting. If an organization meets less often than quarterly, the motion remains on the table until the end of the same meeting (90–91, 214). (See "Postpone to a Certain Time (or Definitely)," pages 45–46.)

Why can't motions be tabled beyond the end of the following meeting?

To table a motion for an extended period would only complicate matters. Once a motion is laid on the table, "no other motion on the same subject is in order that would either conflict with, or present substantially the same question as, the motion that is lying on the table" (214). To lay a motion on the table beyond the next meeting would, in effect, postpone the subject indefinitely.

May a group of business items be laid on the table?

No (211). The same answer applies to the motion to Postpone to a Certain Time (184–85).

May a motion to Lay on the Table be made after debate has been closed?

Yes. Lay on the Table, as the highest ranking subsidiary motion, can be moved "up until the moment of taking the last vote" following adoption of the Previous Question (212).

How is the motion to Lay on the Table misused?

Because the motion to Lay on the Table is not debatable, requires only a majority vote, and has high precedence, members are too often tempted to use it to kill the main motion. This is an improper use of the motion to Lay on the Table and an example of railroading (210, 215–16). If a member opposes a main motion, he should speak and vote against it. To suppress action on a main motion, a member should move to Postpone Indefinitely (which is debatable).

Another misuse of the motion to Lay on the Table occurs when members confuse it with the motion to Postpone to a Certain Time. Often, a member who wishes to postpone a main motion until later in the same meeting or to the following meeting uses the motion to Lay on the Table rather than the proper motion, the motion to Postpone. There is no such thing as the motion "to lay on the table until . . ." (209, 217). (See "Postpone to a Certain Time (or Definitely)," pages 45–47.)

The motion to Lay on the Table is one of the parliamentary motions that is used too often, and hardly ever—in fact, never—properly. Its purpose gives it a unique power, but that power provides the temptation for misuse.

How can the chair prevent the misuse of the motion to Lay on the Table?

It is a hopeless task. Parliamentarians, when teaching or presenting workshops on parliamentary procedure, inevitably include a sermon against the misuse of Lay on the Table. Indeed, we sound more like priests than parliamentarians. The priest would be more successful. In a meeting, for a bored majority, the temptation is too great not to use the motion to Lay on the Table as a motion to kill. *Robert's* warns of the misuses of the motion:

> This motion is commonly misused in ordinary assemblies—in place of the motion to *Postpone Indefinitely*, to *Postpone to a Certain Time*, or other motions. . . .

In ordinary assemblies, the motion to *Lay on the Table* is out of order if the evident intent is to kill or avoid dealing with a measure. (210)

Then *Robert's* repeats the warning:

MISUSES OF THE MOTION . . . the motion to *Lay on the Table* is subject to a number of incorrect uses that should be avoided. It is out of order to move to lay a pending question on the table if there is evidently no other matter requiring immediate attention. . . .

The motion to *Lay on the Table* is often incorrectly used and wrongly admitted as in order with the intention of either killing an embarrassing question without a direct vote, or of suppressing a question without debate. The first of these two uses is unsafe if there is any contest on the issue; the second is in violation of a basic principle of general parliamentary law that only a two-thirds vote can rightfully suppress a main question without allowing free debate. (215–16)

Few members are aware of *Robert's* admonition. No matter. The chair has enough problems without alleging intent about why members are making the motion to Lay on the Table.[46]

When a member, or the chair (211–12), suspects that another member has misused the motion to Lay on the Table, the member may rise to a Parliamentary Inquiry and ask, "Would the maker of the motion care to inform the body of the urgent business that needs to be considered at this time?" Such a tactic may expose the dastardly act—or it may get the member a reputation as the organization's show off.

Granted, there may be that rare situation when the assembly needs the power of the motion to Lay on the Table, but it is clearly a case of arguing the exception—the rare exception—rather than the rule, and the motion to Lay on the Table should be retired.[47]

Instead of using the motion Lay on the Table, the chair can ask, "Given the urgent business that has been called to our attention, is the assembly ready to vote on the pending motion?" If yes, it takes only a few moments to dispose of the pending business. If no, someone can move to close debate. If the motion to close debate is adopted, once again the pending motion is disposed of in a few moments.

Or, after it is known that there is urgent business, someone can move to postpone the pending motion until consideration of the urgent business is completed. The motion to Postpone is debatable, but if a majority of the members cannot see that the urgent business is urgent, maybe it isn't urgent. And, if the urgent business is obviously urgent, then there should be little difficulty in adopting a motion to Postpone. If, for example, a local teachers' association is debating a motion to hold a membership event and word arrives that the school board has just voted to change bargaining rights, or increase class size, or require proof of illness for sick-day leave, the motion to Lay on the Table won't be needed to get to the urgent business.

Take from the Table

Since the motion to Lay on the Table is nearly always misused, is the motion to Take from the Table needed?

No and yes.

No. Because the motion to Lay on the Table is misused either to kill or to postpone the main motion, the motion to Take from the Table is ignored. Because of these misuses, the motion to Lay on the Table should be eliminated, and the motion to Take from the Table would have no choice but to go along.

Yes. The motion to Take from the Table at least provides the opportunity to try to bring back a main motion that was killed by inappropriate use of the motion to Lay on the Table.

How soon, how often, and for how long may a member make the motion to Take from the Table?

How soon after a main motion has been laid on the table may a member make the motion to Take from the Table? A member must wait until "some business or interrupting matter has been transacted or dealt with" (301) before moving to take from the table—usually after one intervening main motion.

How often may a member make the motion to Take from the Table? The motion to Take from the Table may be renewed each time business has been transacted (301, 340, 399).

For how long may a member make the motion to Take from the Table? If the organization meets at least quarterly, the motion to Take from the Table can be made until the end of the following meeting. If the organization does not meet at least quarterly, the motion to Take from the Table can be made only until the end of that same meeting (301–2). (See "Postpone to a Certain Time (or Definitely)," pages 45–46, and "Lay on the Table," page 59.)

What is unique about the precedence of the motion to Take from the Table?

The motion to Take from the Table takes precedence over no pending business. However, after the urgent matter that led to a Lay on the Table motion has been disposed of, the motion to Take from the Table has precedence over any new main motion that another member may seek to present at the same time (300–302). If a member rises to move to take from the table and the chair recognizes another member who wishes to make a new main motion, the member who wants to resume consideration of the tabled motion should inform the chair that she has risen to move to take from the table (302).

What happens to motions that were pending when the main motion was laid on the table?

If the motion to Take from the Table is made at the same meeting in which the main motion was tabled, all pending motions return with the main motion.

If the motion to Take from the Table is made at the following meeting, motions to Limit or Extend the Limits of Debate and to close debate would no longer be pending because motions affecting the limits of debate do not extend beyond the meeting at which they are made (195–96).

May the chair take business from the table?

No. The chair may, however, remind the assembly what motions remain on the table.

Raise a Question of Privilege

For what purpose does one Raise a Question of Privilege?

The purpose is to make an urgent request relating to the rights, privileges, or welfare of the assembly or of individual members (224).

What are the kinds of questions of privilege?

There are two types:

1. questions of privilege of *the assembly,* such as those relating to the physical comfort of the members, and
2. questions of *personal* privilege, such as those relating to changes circulated against a member's character.

Is a question of privilege a request or a motion?

A question of privilege can be either a request or a motion. Usually, the question of privilege is a *request.* For example:

> MEMBER: Mr. Chairman, I rise to a question of privilege of the assembly.
> CHAIR: State your question of privilege.
> MEMBER: May we have the blinds pulled to eliminate the glare of the sun?

Occasionally a *motion* of privilege may be warranted. For example:

> MEMBER: Mr. Chairman, I rise to a question of privilege to present a motion.
> CHAIR: State your motion.
> MEMBER: As a motion of privilege, I move that we go into executive session [a closed meeting] for the discussion of the motion.

Is a question of privilege the device to use to make an announcement or to express appreciation?

No (227). Question of privilege of the member is used more often than question of privilege of the assembly (which is seldom used), but *rarely, if ever, properly.* Listen to Robert himself: "In ordinary societies it is very seldom that a question of personal privilege can arise." And, when Robert was asked whether there are occasions that justify raising a question of personal privilege, he replied: "No. So seldom do they occur that I cannot recall a case in my own experience" (*Parliamentary Law*, 517).

Concerning misuse of the device, Robert continues, "Ninety per cent of the instances of persons rising to a question of personal privilege that I have seen recorded in the proceedings of societies were not questions of privilege" (*Parliamentary Law*, 517). Demeter begins his discussion of the motion: "Grave injustices and countless wrongs have been and are constantly being done both to business and to members because of misuse of this proceeding. The motion to 'raise a question of privilege' is one of the least understood and most abused and misapplied motions in parliamentary law." Demeter later lists the specific abuses: taking the floor away from a speaker; making some explanation or correcting a misstatement uttered in the course of debate; and rising to a Point of Order, to a Request for Information, or to a Parliamentary Inquiry.[48] Hardcastle agrees: "It should not be confused with motions to secure information, or for a parliamentary inquiry."[49] The Opinions Committee of the AIP adds that expressions of appreciation do not fall within the purpose of question of privilege.[50] Regardless, the end of nearly every convention is inundated with delegates rising to questions of personal privilege to make announcements or to express appreciation to someone. After the expression of appreciation for the parliamentarian, the proceedings begin to drag.

And the authorities have not even mentioned the most trying misuse: the member who uses the device to drag the assembly through the member's misery. Take, for instance, the delegate who rises to a question of personal privilege to rant and rave that a friend was treated unfairly by the credentials committee. Of course, the member will not make the appropriate motion to challenge the committee—the member "doesn't want to cause trouble" (translation: the result might not confirm his bitterness)—but just wants to inform the assembly of the injustice.

Robert should have heeded his own experience and eliminated the request and motion to rise to a question of privilege. For requests, Parliamentary Inquiry will do. For motions, an incidental main motion will suffice. For announcements, most meetings include such a heading in the order of business, which precludes the need to interrupt business with an improper question of privilege.

Recess

When is the motion to Recess a privileged motion?

The motion to Recess is privileged only when business is pending. A motion to Recess that is made when no question is pending is a main motion.

Is the motion to Recess debatable?

When a main motion is pending, the motion to Recess is not debatable (230–31). Some authorities allow debate limited to the time duration or to the need for a recess.[51] Robert's allows the privileged motion to Recess to be amended, but not debated (231). The motion to Recess is debatable if it is made when no motion is pending.

What's the difference between ending the day with a recess versus an adjournment at a convention?

There is little difference; in both cases business is taken up where it was interrupted when the motion to Recess or the motion to Adjourn was made. Following an adjournment, however, the following day will begin with opening ceremonies or the reading of minutes (85).

Must a motion to Recess be expressed in an amount of time?

No, a recess can be until the meeting is called to order by the chair or until after some event, such as the arrival of the treasurer (232).

May the assembly recess for a long period of time?

Robert's says a recess is a "short intermission," but there is no definite limitation on the length of a recess except that it cannot extend beyond the time for the next regular or special meeting. The term recess is commonly used for an interval of a few minutes (230).

Adjourn

What are the different forms of the motion to Adjourn?

The motion to Adjourn can be made in either the unqualified or qualified form. "When there is provision for another meeting and no time for adjourning is already set," the unqualified motion to Adjourn, "I move we adjourn," is always a privileged motion and thus undebatable, regardless of whether business is pending (233).[52] In meetings of ordinary societies, seldom will a member use any form other than the unqualified (and privileged) motion "I move we adjourn," and beginners need read no further.

The exceptions to the rule that the motion to Adjourn is a privileged motion and undebatable--when instead it is a main motion and debatable, are:

1. when the motion is qualified in any way, such as to adjourn at or to a future time;
2. when a time for adjourning is already established;
3. or when the effect of the motion to Adjourn, if adopted, would be to dissolve the assembly—adjourn sine die—with no provision for another meeting (such as the last day of a convention). (234)

Is the motion to Adjourn in order while a vote is being taken?

No, but there is an exception. The motion to Adjourn "is not in order while the assembly is engaged in voting or verifying a vote, or before the result of a vote has been announced by the chair, except that, in the case of a vote taken by ballot, a motion to *Adjourn* is in order after the ballots have been collected . . . and before the result has been announced" (235). This exception is music to the ears of delegates who wish to leave for home following a long convention.

May the chair just announce that the meeting is adjourned?

The answer is a qualified yes. In a convention with a scheduled adjournment time in an adopted agenda, no motion to Adjourn is necessary (240–41). Similarly, in a local society with regular meetings, when the order of business has been completed and there is no further business, the chair may state, "Since there is no further business, the meeting is adjourned" (241, 86).

What parliamentary steps are in order while a motion to Adjourn is pending?

1. to notify the assembly of business requiring attention;
2. to make important announcements;
3. to make a motion to Reconsider;
4. to make a motion to Reconsider and Enter on the Minutes;
5. to give notice of a motion requiring previous notice;
6. to move to Fix the Time to Which to Adjourn (238–39).

May the chair call an adjourned meeting back to order?

Yes. *Robert's* provides that if immediately following adjournment, the chair learns that a member was seeking the floor to take certain parliamentary steps, the chair must call the meeting back to order (240).

Fix the Time to Which to Adjourn

What is the purpose of the motion to Fix the Time to Which to Adjourn?

The purpose "is to set the time, and sometimes the place, for another meeting to continue business of the session, with no effect on when the present meeting will adjourn" (242). In other words, the purpose of the motion to Fix the Time to Which to Adjourn is not to adjourn, but to provide the time (and place) to continue the present meeting.

Is the motion to Fix the Time to Which to Adjourn always a privileged motion?

No. "A motion to fix the time to which to adjourn is privileged only when it is made while a question is pending" (242).

What is the form for moving to Fix the Time to Which to Adjourn?

The member states, "I move that, when we adjourn, we adjourn to meet next Monday at 7:00 P.M."

Point of Order

What is the purpose of a Point of Order?

According to *Robert's*, a Point of Order may be raised if the chair

1. overlooks that the rules of the assembly are being violated (247),
2. assigns the floor to the wrong person (31),
3. fails to rule out of order a main motion that is outside the society's objects as defined in the bylaws or constitution (268), or
4. fails to rule out of order a main motion that is outside the announced purpose for which a mass meeting has been announced (268).

A Point of Order, then, is a claim by a member that a specific rule is being or has just been violated and is a demand that the rule be enforced.[53]

On page 49, we suggested that Point of Order can replace the privileged motion to Call for the Orders of the Day. *Robert's* says that Call for the Orders of the Day is used when the chair fails to conform to the "agenda, program, or order of business, or to take up a general or special order that is due to come up at the time" (219), which fits nicely within "when a member thinks that the rules of the assembly are being violated" (247).

If a member is a jealous advocate of proper procedure, it might be wise to adhere to the restraint in *Robert's* advice: "In ordinary meetings it is undesirable to raise points of order on minor irregularities of a purely technical character, if it is clear that no one's rights are being infringed upon and no real harm is being done to the proper transaction of business" (250). Robert originally gave good advice, which is worth repeating:

> It is a mistake to be constantly raising points of order in regard to little irregularities. . . . The assembly meets to transact business, not to have members exploit their knowledge of parliamentary law. A business meeting is not a class in parliamentary law. It is a nuisance to have the time of the assembly wasted by

a member's raising points of order on technical points when no harm is done by the irregularity. (*Parliamentary Law*, 151)

What is the procedure for raising a Point of Order?

MEMBER: I rise to a point of order.
CHAIR: State your point of order.
MEMBER: My point is . . .
CHAIR: The point is [not] well taken and . . .

How soon must a member make the Point of Order?

Immediately. The member *must* make the Point of Order at the time of the violation (250). The rationale is obvious. It would make little sense to rise to a Point of Order fifteen minutes after a speaker's remarks to say that the remarks were not germane to the motion. The damage is long done. *Robert's* even goes so far as to state that "if the chair is stating the question on a motion . . . that is out of order in the existing parliamentary situation, the time to raise [this point] of order is when the chair states the motion. After debate on such a motion has begun—no matter how clearly out of order the motion may be—a point of order is too late" (250). And as stated in *Parliamentary Law*: "After a member has finished his speech, it is too late to call in question the propriety of language used in the earlier part of his speech. After an amendment has been debated it is too late to rule it out of order, even though it is unquestionably not germane" (150).

The general rule that the Point of Order must be made immediately is well taken and should be followed. If, however, debate on an amendment reveals that the intent of the amendment is not germane to the original motion or if a motion is being debated that clearly is out of order in the "existing parliamentary situation," it is customary to allow the Point of Order to be made.

Finally, *Robert's* does provide an exception to the timeliness rule. "The only exceptions . . . arise in connection with breaches that are of a continuing nature, in which case a point of order can be made at any time during the continuance of the breach" (251). *Robert's* lists five instances of such breaches—including an adopted motion that conflicts with the bylaws—and concludes that in such cases, "it is never too late to raise a point of order since any action so taken is null and void" (251).

What confusion often results when a member raises a Point of Order?

Meetings often break down because the chair fails to rule promptly on a Point of Order (69). Once a Point of Order is raised, the chair must rule either "The point is well taken" or "The point is not well taken." *To fail to rule is to fail to lead*, and at this point the meeting dies or turns into a parliamentary quibble. Should the chair hesitate to rule, often another member will rise to a Point of Order about the first Point of Order. In hopes of having the first point clarified, the chair makes the catastrophic mistake of acknowledging the second Point of Order: "My point of order is that the first point of order is out of order." At this moment, the door opens to interminable points of order, and the result will be chaos.

Although there are numerous exceptions, a good guideline to follow is to *allow only one incidental motion on the floor at a time*. Because incidental motions have no order of precedence, trying to deal with more than one incidental motion at a time is confusing. If a second Point of Order or incidental motion is made before the chair has a chance to rule on the first point, the chair should state, "Please hold your point of order until the chair has ruled on the first point."

What if the chair does not know if a Point of Order is well taken?

If the chair is in doubt about the answer to a Point of Order, he should consult the parliamentarian. A good parliamentarian, of course, will already have given guidance to the chair. If the chair is still in doubt, there is an alternative to stating that the point is well taken or not well taken: the chair may submit the Point of Order to a vote of the assembly by saying, "The chair is in doubt and submits the question to the assembly. The question is [for example]: is the speaker's debate germane to the motion?"

When the chair submits a Point of Order to the assembly, the Point of Order becomes debatable, and the chair may enter into the debate (249, 395, 451).

Appeal

What is the purpose of an Appeal from the Decision of the Chair?

If a member disagrees with a decision of the chair, the member may ask that the assembly decide the question. In other words, an Appeal is the assembly's or the member's protection against the tyranny of or, in nearly all cases, an error by the chair (255–56).

What rulings may be appealed?

A *decision* by the presiding officer is generally subject to an Appeal. Remember, the chair's reply to a Parliamentary Inquiry cannot be appealed. The reply is an *opinion*, not a ruling (259).

There are three exceptions to the rule that all decisions by the chair may be appealed:

1. "if a point of order is raised while an appeal is pending, there is no appeal from the chair's decision on this point of order" (256);

2. "when the chair rules on a question about which there cannot possibly be two reasonable opinions, an appeal would be dilatory and is not allowed" (256).

3. "no appeal can be made from a decision of the assembly itself" (254).

This last exception applies to the situation in which the chair turns over a Point of Order to the assembly. (See "Point of Order," page 72).

When may an appeal be made?

The Appeal must be made immediately, at the time of the ruling. If any debate or business has intervened, it is too late to appeal" (257).

Is an Appeal from the decision of the chair debatable?

Yes, usually. An Appeal is not debatable; however, if it "(a) relates to indecorum or a transgression of the rules of speaking; (b) relates to the priority of business; or (c) is made when an undebatable question is immediately pending or involved in the appeal" (257, 398).

What is the procedure for debating the motion to Appeal?

Robert's suggests the following:

1. The chair states the reasons for her ruling.
2. Each member is entitled to speak once.
3. The chair may again state her reasons or answer questions (257–58).

Usually, the member who appeals from the decision states his reasons and the chair state her reasons.

What is unique about the debate on the motion to Appeal?

First, the motion to Appeal is the only motion in which the chair may enter into the debate without relinquishing the chair. (In addition, as stated on page 72, if the chair turns a Point of Order over to the assembly, the chair, as presiding officer, may enter into debate.)

Second, a member may speak only once on an Appeal from the Decision of the Chair. The chair may speak twice (258).

How should the Appeal be stated to the assembly for a vote?

The chair should state, "The question is, 'Shall the decision of the chair be sustained?' Those in favor of sustaining the decision of the chair, say *aye*. Those *opposed* to sustaining the decision of the chair, say *no*." (See the cue card example in "The Parliamentarian," page 150.)

A majority vote in the negative is required to overrule the chair's decision. A tie vote sustains the decision of the chair (258).

May the chair vote on an Appeal?

Yes (258).

May a member criticize a decision of the chair without making an Appeal?

Not according to *Robert's*. "Members have no right to criticize a ruling of the chair unless they appeal from his decision" (256).[54]

What limitation should apply to the use of the motion to Appeal?

Although an Appeal is the motion through which all decisions ultimately reside in the majority will of the assembly, restraint should be exercised in the use of this motion. *Robert's* states, "If a member disagrees with a ruling of the chair affecting any substantial question, he should not hesitate to Appeal. The situation is no more delicate than disagreeing with another member in debate" (258). The key term is "substantial," for failing to exercise restraint with appeals can result in reducing the credibility of the chair, thereby weakening the organization. (See "Parliamentary Inquiry and Request for Information," page 90.)

Suspend the Rules

What rules may be suspended?

The regular procedural rules of the assembly may be suspended. *Regular procedural rules* mean

1. rules contained in the parliamentary authority,
2. special rules of order, or
3. standing rules. (261)

What rules may not be suspended?

The assembly may not suspend what it does not control, such as the bylaws (or constitution); local, state, or national law; or fundamental principles of parliamentary law (260, 263–65). For example, rules protecting absentees cannot be suspended even by a unanimous vote because the absentees do not consent to the suspension.

Are there exceptions to the rule that bylaws cannot be suspended?

Yes, there are two exceptions. Bylaw clauses occasionally provide for their own suspension (17, 263). In addition, "Rules clearly identifiable as in the nature of rules of order that are placed within the bylaws can . . . also be suspended by a two-thirds vote" (17). An example would be when an organization places its order of business in the bylaws (17).

What must the motion to Suspend the Rules contain?

The motion to Suspend the Rules must contain the specific purpose for suspending the rules. Its adoption permits nothing else to be done under the suspension (262).

Robert's prefaces the discussion of what the motion should contain with the statement that "the particular rule or rules to be suspended are not mentioned" (262). Ignore this advice. If the purpose, for example, is to suspend or amend a particular standing or special rule of a convention, it is consistent with the general requirement of specificity and clarity when making motions to include the specific rule to be suspended. There is no harm in stating, "I move to suspend Standing Rule 4-B for the purpose of . . ."

What vote is required to suspend the rules?

A two-thirds vote is usually required, but the answer is more complicated than many realize. The complications are twofold.

First, organizations often—in fact, usually—do not distinguish between standing rules and special rules. They combine both within standing rules. When an organization combines standing and special rules, a two-thirds vote is required to adopt the standing rules. (For help in distinguishing between standing and special rules, see 15–18, 87–88, 263–66, and 620–21).

Second, there is a little-known principle that prevents suspension of a rule by a negative vote that is as great as the minority protected by the rule. Therefore, the vote required to suspend the rules will vary as set out below.

1. A two-thirds vote is required to suspend rules of parliamentary procedure, or what Robert's calls rules of order.

> The *rules of order* of a society, as contained in the manual established by the bylaws as the parliamentary authority, or as included in any special rules of order adopted by the organization, are rules of parliamentary procedure, the suspension of which requires a two-thirds vote. Some societies call all their rules "standing rules." But by whatever name a rule is called, if it relates to parliamentary procedure, it requires either (a) previous notice and a two-thirds vote or (b) a vote of a majority of the entire membership for its amendment; hence it requires a two-thirds vote for its suspension. (265)

2. A majority vote is required to suspend rules relating to the administration of an organization, such as setting the hour at which meetings are to begin. *Robert's* calls these standing rules.

> *Standing rules*, as understood in [*Robert's*] except in the case of conventions, are rules (1) which are related to the details of the administration of a society rather than to parliamentary procedure, and (2) which can be adopted or changed upon the same conditions as any ordinary act of the society. . . .

> Standing rules are adopted, as any ordinary motion, by a majority vote, and they may be amended by a majority vote with previous notice; they therefore can be suspended by a majority vote as they do not involve the protection of a minority of a particular size. (18, 265–66)

In summary, rules such as those that limit debate or establish an order of business are special rules and require a two-thirds vote to suspend; rules such as those prohibiting the use of cellphones or the distribution of campaign materials are standing rules and require a majority vote to suspend.

With the distinction between special and standing rules clarified, we turn to the other complication, the little-known principle of minority protection.

3. A negative vote that is less than the minority being protected by a rule is required for the suspension of that rule. *Robert's* provides that "no rule protecting a minority of a particular size can be suspended in the face of a negative vote as large as the minority protected by the rule" (261).[55] The best way to clarify this principle is to review the reasoning behind why an assembly cannot go from a ballot vote to an open vote. (See "Voting," page 132.) Since rules protecting absentees or the basic rights of individual members cannot be suspended even by a unanimous vote, and since the rule requiring an election by ballot protects a minority of one from exposing her vote (which the member may do if she votes against suspending the requirement of voting by ballot), it follows that an assembly cannot go from a secret ballot to an open vote (263, 412–13, 441–43, 573).

The rationale for previous notice provides a second example. As explained on page 27, the rule requiring previous notice of a proposed amendment to the bylaws protects an absent member who decided not to attend the meeting because there had been no notice of amendments to the bylaws. To allow a suspension of previous notice at the meeting to consider an amendment to the bylaws would circumvent the purpose of giving notice (263). In each case, the principle of protecting a minority has been applied, and, since in each case the protection is for a single member, the rule cannot be suspended.

To conclude this discussion of what vote is required, the answer is *usually two-thirds*, but be aware of the distinction between rules of order and standing rules and of the principle of minority protection.

How is the suspension of convention rules different?

Convention standing rules are ordinarily adopted by a two-thirds vote (619–20). Once adopted, a convention standing rule can be suspended for a specific purpose by a majority vote (620–21). To suspend both the convention rule and any applicable *Robert's* rule requires a two-thirds vote (621).

How often may members try to suspend the same rule for the same purpose at the same meeting?

Once, unless unanimous consent is given (262).

What is the "Gordian Knot" motion?

The Standard Code recognizes an interesting use of Suspend the Rules when "the parliamentary situation in a meeting becomes so confused that neither the chair nor the members can figure out how to proceed." In such circumstances, suspend the rules can be used to "cancel out everything that has been done" and allow the body to restart the motion with a clean slate.[56]

Objection to the Consideration of a Question

What is the purpose of an Objection to the Consideration of a Question?

The purpose is to prevent the assembly from considering an original main motion. Recall that the purpose of the motion to call for the Previous Question is to close, not to prevent, debate. If a member wishes to prevent all discussion and consideration of a motion, objection to consideration should be used (391).

What justifies preventing debate on an original main motion?

The answer in *Robert's* is that objection to consideration may be used when the assembly believes "it would be strongly undesirable for the motion even to come before the assembly" (267). *Robert's* does make it clear when it should not be used: "If a main motion is outside the society's objects as defined in the bylaws or constitution, or outside the announced purpose for which a mass meeting has been called; such [an improper] motion should be ruled out of order" (268).[57]

What limitations apply in objecting to consideration?

First, Objection to the Consideration of a Question applies only to original main motions (103, 268). Second, the objection must be made before debate has begun on the original main motion.

Does Objection to Consideration require a second?

Robert's says that no second is required (268).

How does the chair present the motion to the assembly for a vote?

The chair states, "There is an objection to the consideration of Ms. Y's main motion. The question is: shall Ms. Y's main motion be considered? Those in favor of considering the main motion, please stand. Those opposed to considering the main motion, please stand."

This format, like the wording of an Appeal, appears to be in reverse, but for good reason. Any other form will probably confuse the assembly about what motion is being voted on. (*Robert's* wording is slightly different and not as clear.) And remember, it takes a two-thirds vote in the negative for an Objection to the Consideration of a Question to be sustained (268).

This form for putting the question is based on the principle that a member has a right to present a motion in a democratic society; thus, those who wish to deny this right are the objectors. The vote is whether to affirm this right or to deny this right. (See "Appeal," page 74, for the same principle.)

If an Objection to the Consideration of a Question is sustained (receives a two-thirds vote in the negative), for how long is the main motion dead?

The main motion is dismissed for that session (269). Although it is commonplace to refer to objection to consideration as a motion to be adopted or rejected, *Robert's* treats an objection to consideration as a request, and thus the proper announcement is whether the objection is or is not sustained.

May a member use Point of Order in place of objection to consideration?

Yes. Without any loss of the organization's right to protect itself from contentious motions, Point of Order can do the job of objection to consideration. *Robert's* says that object to consideration is similar to Point of Order (268). Also, placing the responsibility for the purpose of objection to consideration under Point of Order will prevent the misuse of such purpose by placing the decision "up front." For whatever reason, any decision to rule a motion out of order is the responsibility of the chair—the leader. "It is the duty of the presiding officer to prevent members from misusing the legitimate forms of motions" (342), and the chair should be prepared to provide a specific and clear reason for the ruling. The same holds for any member who rises to a Point of Order to state that a motion should not be in order.

One might think that dropping from a motion that requires a two-thirds vote to a procedure (chair's ruling or Point of Order subject to Appeal) that requires only a tie vote weakens the protection for the maker of the motion. Numerically it does; but by placing the decision up front, it is unlikely that any motion, unless clearly and overwhelmingly objectionable, will be ruled out of order. A myth prevails that chairs are tyrants who love to suppress the rights of the grassroots members. The opposite is generally true. Chairs are usually if anything, obsessed with bending over backward to be fair, to ensure that each member has an opportunity to have his or her say—sometimes at the expense of the convention's valuable time.

In addition to the temptation for misuse, the distinction between original main motions (which may be objected to) and incidental main motions (which may not be objected to) can be complicated. Read, for example, in Robert's *Parliamentary Law*:

> Incidental main questions, as the report of a committee on a subject upon which it has been ordered to report, or an amendment to the bylaws, cannot be objected to, but the report or opinions of a minority of a committee may be objected to. The report of a committee which it has not been ordered to make can be objected to, just as any other original main motion. The consideration of petitions and communications from members or subordinate organizations may be objected to, but not communications from a superior organization. (155)

When one thinks about it, each of these distinctions makes sense. But in the large task of preparing delegates to be effective and responsible representatives in their deliberative organizations, the distinctions and the motion itself are not worth the effort.

It is probably fortunate that most people are unaware of objection to consideration. Given its broad purpose, there is little doubt that it would be misused. During one workshop following the explanation of objection to consideration, we added, "But you will never see an objection used." In the late-evening hours of the next convention, after the chair stated that "Resolution 123 is now before the assembly," out of the assembly came, "Madam President, I object to the consideration of the resolution." Sure enough, in the back of the hall stood the president of the local unit—with a wink and a grin. The objection was sustained. Before the meeting recessed for the evening (early morning), more than one resolution went the way of a sustained objection to consideration. The next day, delegates were commenting about how they had found a new way to move through a large number of resolutions. Any parliamentarian would have been hard pressed to advise the chair that any of the motions to object to consideration were in order.

Division of a Question (Divide a Motion)

To what motions may the motion to divide a question be applied?

Robert's states that the motion to divide a motion applies to main motions and their amendments, although for most situations the division will apply to main motions (271). For all practical purposes, the answer is main motions.

What limitation applies to the making of the motion to divide a motion?

The main motion must be divisible. The answer sounds obvious, but this requirement is often overlooked. The rule is that a motion cannot be divided if each division cannot stand by itself. "A motion cannot be divided unless each part presents a proper question for the assembly to act upon if none of the other parts is adopted" (272). For example, the motion "I move we assess each member $50 and give that money to the political action committee" is not divisible because the second half, "give that money to the political action committee," cannot stand alone. If the first part, "assess each member $50," is rejected, there is no second part.

What vote is required to divide a motion?

If all of the parts of the motion relate to the same subject, then the motion to divide requires a majority vote (110, 272). If any of the parts of the motion relate to different subjects (such as a committee report with a series of independent resolutions offered in one motion), then the motion must be divided at the demand of a single member.

So, remember the distinction: same subject, majority vote; different subjects, demand of one member.

What is the procedure involved in dividing a motion?

Although it is possible to disagree on the ways in which a particular motion might be divided, the motion to divide a motion usually involves little formality and is arranged by unanimous consent.

Consideration by Paragraph or Seriatim

What does "consider seriatim" mean?

To *consider seriatim* means to consider a motion part by part. (Literally, *seriatim* means "in a series," so a motion could be considered by sentence, paragraph, or section.)

What is the difference between the motion to divide and the motion to consider by paragraph or seriatim?

When a motion is divided, it becomes two (or more) main motions that are separate in every way. When a motion is considered part by part, it remains on the floor as one main motion. Thus, in effect, there are two differences:

1. If a motion is divided, the assembly debates and votes on each division separately. If the parts of the motion are considered individually (seriatim), no vote is taken until all parts have been discussed. When considering by part, amendments are voted on as they arise, but no part as amended is voted on at that time.

2. If a motion is divided, a motion to Postpone Indefinitely, Refer, Postpone, or Lay on the Table applies only to the main motion that is being discussed. If the assembly is considering the motion part by part, any motion to Postpone Indefinitely, Refer, Postpone, or Lay on the Table applies to the entire series (279).

When would an assembly consider a "motion by paragraph"?

The motion to consider by paragraph is helpful when adopting or revising bylaws, when considering planks in a platform, or when a committee recommendation consists of several parts (276–77). As stated earlier, *seriatim* means in a series; thus, the division need not necessarily be by paragraph.

What is the procedure for Consideration by Paragraph?

If the assembly agrees to consider a motion by paragraph, follow these guidelines:

1. The member who moved the adoption of the document (such as the chair of the bylaws committee), the secretary, or the chair reads the first subdivision, which is then explained by its proponent.

2. The chair then asks, "Is there debate or amendment to this part?" A member may speak twice on each part. Thus, debate during consideration seriatim is an exception to the rule of twice on each motion (277).

3. When there is no further debate or amendment to the first part, steps 1 and 2 are repeated for each succeeding part.

4. After all parts have been considered, the chair opens the entire document to amendment. At this time, additional parts may be inserted, parts may be struck, or any one of them may be further amended.

5. The entire document is acted upon in a single vote (278–79).

What can be done to end debate on one part so the assembly can move on to the next part?

According to *Robert's*, nothing can be done: "*The Previous Question* and *Limit or Extend Limits of Debate* can be applied to amendments or to the entire document but not to the individual paragraphs" (279). In theory, the rule makes sense. If members are against the paragraph, they will amend by striking it; if members are in favor of the paragraph, they will remain quiet and move on to the next paragraph. In practice, however, delegates at large conventions often continue to debate the merits of the paragraph; and, in this case, the rule forbidding the motion to close debate is ignored or, in effect, suspended or an actual motion to Suspend the Rules and move to the next paragraph will be made.

Division of the Assembly

What is the purpose of the call for a Division of the Assembly?

The purpose is to check the accuracy of a voice vote by requesting that the vote be retaken by rising.

Does the chair have to recognize a call for a Division of the Assembly?

Yes. Well, nearly always: "When it is clear that there has been a full vote and there can be no reasonable doubt as to which side is in the majority, a call for a *Division* is dilatory, and the chair should not allow the individual member's right of demanding a *Division* to be abused to the annoyance of the assembly" (282). On this one, the chair better be certain the request is dilatory or, better yet, gather the evidence for the annoyers to defeat themselves: Three times on the first day of a convention a vocal minority demanded a Division of the Assembly on votes for which there could be no doubt. The chair permitted each. On day two, when these members again requested a Division on a vote that was clearly adopted, the chair stated, "Yesterday on three occasions the chair granted the request for a Division on votes that clearly received more than a majority vote. The chair believes this vote was clearly adopted and rules the request for a Division to be dilatory." Thunderous applause. The chair invested time on the first day of the convention in order to save time on the following two days of the convention. Moral of the story: Allow the poor losers enough rope to hang themselves.

May a member simply request that the vote be retaken?

Yes. Call for a Division of the Assembly (or house) is an archaic expression, and *Robert's* says that a member may state simply, "Division," or, "I call for [or 'demand'] a Division," or, "I doubt the result of the vote" (52, 282). The chair should recognize any expression (such as "I request that the vote be retaken") that is clearly a request to take the vote again.

How soon may a member call for a Division of the Assembly?

A member can demand a Division "from the moment the negative votes have been cast" (52, 281–82). However, a member should be cautioned against a hasty call for a Division. It can be embarrassing to hear the chair say, "Gee, the chair was just going to state the vote in your favor." It is best to remain calm and wait until the chair announces the vote.

When is it too late to call for a Division of the Assembly?

Robert's 10th edition permitted a Division "until, but not after, *the chair has stated the question* on another motion." The 11th Edition has narrowed this window by only allowing a Division to be called "until the announcement of the result is complete, or immediately thereafter" (52, 281).

As a general rule, limiting the time to call for a Division is well taken; but if interpreted literally, it provides a temptation for a chair to railroad a motion through by rushing to the next item of business. Also, in conventions, it takes delegates a short but reasonable amount of time to get to a microphone (to hold up a card) or to call in a request for a Division. (Delegates usually try to follow the convention rule that a speaker must go to a microphone, and they are thus not aware that they can simply yell, "Division," from their seats.) Fortunately, the authors of the 11th Edition added a new paragraph saying that it is too late to demand a division "after any member has been recognized and begun to speak in debate or to give a report or presentation, or after the chair has stated the question on a subsequently made motion, or after the chair has begun to take the vote and any member has voted on another motion that was pending" (409). The new language provides the chair with the flexibility to ensure that members, especially convention delegates, have an opportunity to call for a division.

Other than challenging the vote, why might a member call for a Division?

According to the Opinions Committee of the American Institute of Parliamentarians, there are several proper purposes for asking for a Division even when the vote was clear, including:

1. "to try to obtain a unanimous decision,
2. to try to obtain a larger, more representative vote,
3. to see how others voted, and
4. to avoid the impression that the vote was railroaded."[58]

Also, since the visual vote eliminates some degree of anonymity, the Division may change some members' votes.

May a member Appeal the announcement of a vote rather than call for a Division of the Assembly?

No, a Division refers *only* to a verification of the vote; an Appeal refers to a decision of the chair. Occasionally, a member believes that the chair has made a mistake in the count of a vote, and, in error, the member rises to Appeal from the Decision of the Chair. The chair's announcement of the vote, however, is not a decision; the proper request is to call for a Division of the Assembly (259).

If a Division is requested, how should the vote be taken?

According to *Robert's*, the vote must be a standing vote. "A voice vote retaken by a show of hands is not a *Division of the Assembly*, since in large assemblies it may be less accurate than a rising vote, and since—even in a small meeting—the rising vote may be more effective in causing a maximum number of members to vote" (52, 280).

Although going from a voice vote to a show of hands is technically not a Division, often the second vote is taken by a show of hands, and *Robert's* acknowledges such a procedure:

> On an inconclusive voice vote in a very small meeting where all present can clearly see one another, if, instead of calling for a *Division*, a member asks for a show of hands, this is in the nature of a request, and the chair can retake the vote by this method unless a call for a *Division* is also made. Before or after the vote is thus retaken, however, any member still has the right to demand a *Division* if he believes it will obtain a more conclusive result. (280)

Reading these two passages together as they appear in *Robert's* provides an example of why some consider *Robert's* unduly complex. Demeter, for example, ignores the requirement that a Division requires a standing vote.[59] If the chair wishes to adhere to *Robert's*, the chair should move directly to a standing vote any time there is a call for a Division of the Assembly.

May a Division of the Assembly be called following a rising vote?

No, only following a voice vote or a vote by show of hands (281).

May a member demand that the vote be taken by a particular method?

No, except that, by definition, a Division is a demand to retake a voice vote or a show-of-hands vote by a standing vote (52). A member who wishes a counted vote must move to have the vote taken by count, by roll call, or by ballot; the motion is undebatable and requires a majority vote (unless, of course, provided for specifically in the bylaws or special rules).[60]

Requests and Inquiries

Parliamentary Inquiry and Request for Information

What are the purposes of and what is the difference between a Parliamentary Inquiry and a Request for Information?

A Parliamentary Inquiry is a question "on a matter of parliamentary law or the rules of the organization bearing on the business at hand" (293); a Request for Information is a question about "information relevant to the business at hand but not related to parliamentary procedure" (294). An example of a Parliamentary Inquiry: "Is a motion to amend the pending motion in order at this time?" An example of a Request for Information: "Are there sufficient funds in our budget to cover the cost of this proposal?" Thus, for information concerning procedure, use Parliamentary Inquiry; for information about content, use Request for Information.

What happened to "Point of Information"?

A significant change in the 11th Edition is that Request for Information, rather than "Point of Information," is now the preferred method of asking a question (in hopes that members will understand they should use it to request information, not to provide information, which can stray into debate).

What is the difference between a Parliamentary Inquiry and a Point of Order?

A Parliamentary Inquiry is a question directed to the chair to which the chair gives an *opinion*; a Point of Order is used to call to the attention of the assembly a violation of the rules to which the chair makes a *decision*, a *ruling*.

Is the chair's reply to a Parliamentary Inquiry subject to an Appeal?

No. A reply is an opinion, not a ruling (259, 294). If a member disagrees with the chair's opinion, he can either rephrase his question into a Point of Order or act contrary to the opinion and, if ruled out of order, Appeal from the decision (294).[61]

How does a member raise a Request for Information?

MEMBER: (*rises without obtaining the floor*) Mr. Chairman, I have a request for information.

CHAIR: The member will state her question.

MEMBER: Does the present budget include funds for the project?

May a member raise a Request for Information after a motion to close debate is adopted?

Unfortunately, *Robert's* says "yes." Make that a very qualified yes. Requests for Information are an incidental motion. *Robert's* notes that the "adoption of an order for the *Previous Question* does not prevent the making of privileged or incidental motions" (198). Elsewhere, *Robert's* states that the motion for the Previous Question "yields to the subsidiary motion to *Lay on the Table*, to all privileged motions, and to all applicable incidental motions" (198). This makes some sense, in that a proper Request for Information may help a member decide how to vote, even following the close of debate.

However, large conventions have different concerns, and Requests for Information can easily get out of hand. In a convention of five thousand, even 1 percent of the delegates wanting to ask a question would mean fifty Requests for Information. Moreover, such questions are often thinly veiled questions more in the nature of debate ("Isn't it true that this proposal will cost the union a bazillion dollars?"). Other Requests for Information simply give the maker of a proposal additional opportunities to address the substance of the motion. If this all takes place *after* a vote to close debate, there will be many irate delegates.

In such a setting, there are good arguments as to why Requests for Information should not be permitted after the close of debate:

- The closing of debate signifies that the body is ready to vote on the business at hand and not address additional requests "for information relevant to the business at hand" (294).

- *Robert's* notes that on a Request for Information, "If the speaker consents to the interruption, the time consumed will be taken out of his allowed time" (295). After the Previous Question has been ordered, there is no "allowed time," and a Request for Information should not be permitted to create additional time by allowing the maker to respond to questions.

• Answering a Request for Information (particularly if incorrectly answered) may necessitate a response, which is inappropriate after debate has been closed.

• A Request for Information is different from most incidental motions, in that the others generally must be moved, are undebatable, and require a vote of the body before action. Requests for Information allow a single individual out of thousands to delay the process with no vote of the body.

• Requests for Information can be distinguished from Parliamentary Inquiries in that the former involve the substance of the proposal, and substantive discussion of the motion has been closed through the Previous Question.

• Unless adoption of the Previous Question closes off Requests for Information, there is no easy parliamentary means for the body to get to the vote just ordered without additional motions and votes.

• Requiring a motion to Suspend the Rules to end debate and Requests for Information or a special rule of order that allows the Previous Question to stop Requests for Information seems unnecessarily complicated procedurally.

So, what's the best course of action if Requests for Information are being abused? Well, the chair has several responsibilities, including to "expedite business in every way compatible with the rights of members" (450). Inherent in this right would be to refuse to recognize Requests for Information that have become duplicative, dilatory, or disrupt the proceedings. The worst that likely could happen is that a member could appeal such a decision, which would be decided by a majority vote of the body. Another approach the chair could take would be to permit Requests for Information that are answerable by the chair, but to prohibit Requests for Information that require information from the maker or other delegates (which sounds like more debate). Finally, if Requests for Information regularly get out of hand after the close of debate, it might be worth considering a convention rule that limits or prohibits Requests for Information in certain circumstances.

May a member raise a Request for Information after voting begins?

No. (See "Voting," page 130.)

Is Request for Information the device a member uses to ask the speaker a question?

According to *Robert's*, yes (294–95). This tactic, however, is easily abused and should be used sparingly. The speaker should remember that consenting to the interruption means the time consumed will be taken from his allowed debating time.

May a Request for Information be used to make a point in debate?

A Request for Information should be a question to which the maker doesn't already know the answer. However, *Robert's* concludes the treatment of Request for Information with an unfortunate paragraph: "An inquiry of this kind may also be for the purpose of reminding a speaker of a point to be made in argument, or it may be intended to rebut his position; but it must always be put in the form of a question" (295). The statement invites abuse.

What are the most common abuses of Requests for Information?

The new name, Request for Information, may solve some of the problems that plagued its predecessor, Point of Information (see preceding question). Abuses of Point of Information included using it:

1. to provide a "point" of information in debate, rather than ask a question.

2. to ask a question the asker already knew the answer to, as a form of debate.

3. to keep members from having to do their homework. (Question: "How much will this project cost?" Answer: "The cost will be $40,000, as was discussed at the resolutions open hearing.") Members and delegates should be prepared and not wait until a motion is on the floor to get their questions answered.

4. after the close of debate to make thinly veiled arguments (pro or con) through a question.

Such abuses were especially conspicuous at conventions with card- or phone-system recognition systems to determine the order of speakers, in that questions are typically recognized ahead of debate. Under the old motion, nothing was more arrogant or rude than using points of information to jump over those waiting to debate only to then ask an improper Point of Information. It happened all too often in conventions.[62]

While the new name might solve all these problems, we have our doubts. If Requests for Information are a problem, these are some possible solutions:

1. Suspend the rules to end debate and Requests for Information.

2. Adopt a convention rule that allows adoption of the Previous Question to stop Requests for Information.

3. Use the inherent authority of the chair to "protect the assembly from obviously dilatory motions by refusing to recognize them" and to "enforce the rules relating to debate and those relating to order and decorum" by calling such members to order (450).

May Parliamentary Inquiry be used for purposes other than requesting information about procedure?

Yes, Parliamentary Inquiry is a handy tool of parliamentary procedure and should be used more often:

1. in place of a question of privilege to make a request relating to the rights and privileges of the assembly or any of its members. Requests should be limited to the physical comfort and welfare of the members, such as smoking in the assembly hall, adjusting the heat or air conditioning, correcting the sound system, or reducing the noise in the hallways. (See "Raise a Question of Privilege," page 64.)

2. in place of call for the orders of the day to inquire if the assembly is following its agenda, program, or order of business. (See "Call for the Orders of the Day," page 49.)

3. when in doubt as to which motion to use or just plain lost, confused, or befuddled. Robert assigned this use to Parliamentary Inquiry with the caution, "A member has no right to ask a question on parliamentary law unless it is necessary in order to guide him in his actions at that time" (*Parliamentary Law*, 172). Within this limitation, when nothing seems to make sense, a member may raise a Parliamentary Inquiry: "Madam President, I'm lost, I'm lost; please help me." And someone will help. It might even be the parliamentarian.

Is there any strategic value in the use of Parliamentary Inquiry?

Yes. A member who feels that the chair has made an error may rise to a Point of Order, which means that the member disagrees with the chair. Because Points of Order seem harsher and can weaken the credibility of the chair, the member might use Parliamentary Inquiry to ask if the chair is sure the procedure is correct. For example, a member believes that a speaker's debate is out of order and raises a Parliamentary Inquiry, "Is the speaker's debate germane to the amendment?" Indirect suggestion is often preferable to confrontation. (See "Appeal," pages 74–75.)

Modify or Withdraw a Motion

Who may request permission to withdraw or modify a motion?

Only the maker of the original motion may request permission to withdraw or modify that motion. Any member may suggest that the proposer ask permission to withdraw it (297).

May the assembly require a maker to withdraw his or her motion?

No. "Any member can suggest that the maker of a motion ask permission to withdraw it, which the maker can do or decline to do, as he chooses" (297).

May the maker of a motion modify or withdraw that motion without the permission of the body?

The answer to this question relates to the importance of having the chair state all motions to the assembly, "It is moved and seconded that . . ." Until a motion has been presented to the assembly by the chair, the maker of the motion may modify or withdraw it without anyone's consent. After the motion has been stated by the chair, the proposer may modify or withdraw it only with the permission of the assembly. In other words, as long as the maker of the motion owns the motion, she may do with it as she wishes; once the assembly owns the motion, the maker must obtain the permission of the assembly (40, 114, 295–98).

If the maker of a motion requests permission to modify or withdraw, does the chair ask for the permission of the person who seconded the motion?

No (40). This misconception is common. As stated above, *before* the chair states the motion, a request to modify or withdraw is a demand because the maker of the motion still owns the motion and may do with it as she wishes. *After* the chair states the motion, a request to modify or withdraw requires unanimous consent or a majority vote. The member who seconded the motion has no more control over it than does any other member. Like any other member, the seconder may, of course, object to unanimous consent and may, therefore, require a vote be taken on the request.

What if the maker of the motion wishes to withdraw or modify but some members do not agree?

To withdraw or modify a motion after it has become the property of the assembly, the maker of the motion rises:

> MEMBER: Mr. Chairman, I request permission to withdraw my motion.
>
> CHAIR: Ms. Y requests permission to withdraw her motion. If there is no objection, Ms. Y's motion will be withdrawn. (*Pause*)
>
> MEMBER: Objection.
>
> CHAIR: There is an objection. The question is: Shall permission be granted to withdraw the motion? Those in favor of allowing Ms. Y to withdraw her motion, say "Aye." Those opposed to having the motion withdrawn, say "No."

If the chair does not immediately place the question before the assembly, any member other than the one making the request may move that permission to withdraw the motion be granted (297).

If a majority votes to continue consideration of the motion, the request to withdraw is denied. If there is an objection to a request to modify a motion, the chair must determine whether an amendment or equivalent to the requested modification would be in order. If not, modification may not be made unless a motion to Suspend the Rules is made and adopted. If a motion for such an amendment is in order, the chair can assume it or any member can move it formally (297–98).

How is a "friendly amendment" related to a request to modify a motion?

A friendly amendment is nothing more than a member's suggestion that the maker of the motion request permission to modify it after it has been stated by the chair. If a member moves a friendly amendment, the chair directs the suggested modification to the maker of the motion:

> CHAIR: Does the maker of the motion wish to modify his motion?
> MAKER: Yes.
> CHAIR: If there is no objection, the motion will be modified. Is there objection? (*Pause*) There being no objection, the modification is granted.

If there is objection, the chair states, "The modification is not accepted and therefore must be moved as an amendment" (see 162 and 298).

Are there any motions that cannot be withdrawn?

No, provided the withdrawal is made before it is too late for the motion to be renewed. Thus, the motion to Reconsider cannot be withdrawn after it is too late for anyone else to make the motion (297).

Until when may a motion be withdrawn?

A motion may be withdrawn any time before "voting on the question has begun," even if the motion has been amended or other motions are immediately pending (297).

At a convention, new business items often require the signatures of more than one delegate in order to be submitted. When several signatures are required, who may request permission to modify or withdraw the motion?

If there is a deadline for the submission of new business items, those delegates who wish to withdraw their signatures should inform the chair; and if those requesting to withdraw bring the total below the required number, the chair should ask if any other delegates wish to join the petition. If delegates sufficient to the number required volunteer, the motion is in order. If not, the motion is ruled out of order.

If a deadline for submission of new business items has passed, the motion is the property of the assembly, and the chair rules the motion in order. Once the motion is on the floor, only the member who moved the motion may request permission to withdraw it. Any delegate, of course, including the other signers, may object; and the question would be decided by a vote of the assembly. Organizations that require multiple signatures for motions may want to provide an answer in their special rules.[63]

It is *not* proper for the chair to consider the first name on the list the maker of the motion, thus allowing that person to request permission to withdraw.

At a convention, how does a delegate who submitted a motion prior to the deadline change the motion before it is considered by the assembly?

The delegate requests permission to modify the motion. It is not unusual for delegates to prepare new business items just prior to the deadline for submitting them only to discover later that the motions were poorly written. To improve the motions and to expedite the business of the assembly, three steps should be taken:

1. Prior to the time the motion will be considered by the assembly, the delegate informs the chair in writing of the modification.

2. When the time arrives to consider the motion, the chair informs the assembly of the request to modify, states the modification, and asks if there is objection. (Once the deadline for submitting motions is past, the maker of the motion must obtain the permission of the assembly to modify.)

3. If there is no objection, the chair states the motion as modified. If there is objection, the chair states the original motion, and the maker—or any delegate—can move to amend. (In large conventions with a demanding agenda, if there is objection to a request to modify, by custom the chair goes directly to a vote on whether to grant permission to modify.)

Delegates often make the mistake of waiting until the motion is before the assembly and then moving to amend the motion. Asking the chair in advance to request the modification expedites the business of the assembly.

Rescind or Amend Something Previously Adopted

What is the purpose of the motion to Rescind?

The motion to Rescind is used to nullify or negate a main motion adopted earlier. "The effect of *Rescind* is to strike out an entire main motion, resolution, order, or rule that has been adopted at some previous time" (305).

After a main motion has been adopted, how soon, how often, and for how long may a member make a motion to Rescind?

How soon? Technically, a member may move to rescind immediately, but the practical answer is at the next meeting. Rescind picks up where Reconsider leaves off. At the meeting during which the action was taken, use Reconsider; at the following (or a later) meeting, use Rescind.[64]

How often may a member make the motion to Rescind? A general principle of parliamentary law is that an assembly should not have to consider the same subject matter more than once during a single meeting. (Reconsider is, of course, the exception.) Thus, the answer is once each meeting.

For how long? Theoretically a member may make the motion to Rescind forever (307), but there is a practical limitation: a motion to Rescind cannot cancel or countermand an action that already has been executed.

May part of a previously adopted motion be rescinded?

Yes, there are three routes available for rescinding part of an action that had been adopted previously:

1. At the same meeting, move to reconsider the vote on the main motion that was previously adopted. If the motion to Reconsider is adopted, move to amend by striking.

2. Move to rescind the previously adopted motion, then move to amend the motion to Rescind so that the rescission is limited to part of the motion previously adopted.

3. Move to Amend Something Previously Adopted. This is the most direct route to use "if it is desired to change only a part of the text, or to substitute a different version" (305). The motion to Amend Something Previously Adopted is seldom used and appears to be an exception to the general rule that amendments apply to pending motions. If the motion changes or strikes part of the motion previously adopted, it amends the motion; if the motion strikes the entire motion, it rescinds the motion.

What is the vote required for the motion to Rescind or to Amend Something Previously Adopted?

It depends. A majority vote is required if previous notice is given. If previous notice is not given, then the motion requires a two-thirds vote or a vote of a majority of the entire membership (306–7). (In the unlikely event of the motion in committee, see *Robert's* 306 for the vote requirement.)

Reconsider

What is the purpose of the motion to Reconsider?

The purpose of reconsidering a vote "is to permit correction of hasty, ill-advised, or erroneous action, or to take into account added information or a changed situation that has developed since the taking of the vote" (315). The motion to Reconsider "enables a majority in an assembly, within a limited time and without notice, to bring back for further consideration a motion which has already been voted on" (315).

A principle of parliamentary law is that an assembly cannot be asked to consider the same subject more than once per meeting (336). It is the balance between individual and majority rights. To protect individual rights, if a member chooses to do so, an assembly must put up with the same main motion meeting after meeting; but, to protect the rights of the majority, the member may make the motion only once per meeting.

Obviously, members who lose should not be allowed to waste the time of the entire assembly with repeated efforts to consider the same issue. But people make mistakes. Unfortunately, some of those mistakes are made in meetings, so a motion to Reconsider is an exception to the principle of once per meeting.

Which motions may be reconsidered?

Robert's says that Reconsider "can be applied to the vote on any motion except" and then lists seven principles that provide for exceptions (318–19) and thirty-six votes on motions that cannot be reconsidered (Charts, Tables, and Lists 46–47). The treatment of the motion to Reconsider is one of the most difficult sections in *Robert's*. *The Standard Code* and Keesey simplify by limiting the motion to Reconsider to main motions only. Most of the time, the motion to Reconsider is applied to main motions.

Who may make the motion to Reconsider?

Only a member who voted on the prevailing side may move to Reconsider. *Robert's* sees this limitation as a protection against its dilatory use by a defeated minority. Also, it makes sense to assume that, unless at least one member of the prevailing side has had a change of mind, the motion to Reconsider would be a waste of time.

Some authorities say that the limitation causes more problems than it prevents and that no member should be penalized for the way he or she votes; they allow any member to make the motion to Reconsider. *The Standard Code* summarizes the case against the requirement of having voted on the prevailing side:

1. Any member could vote on the prevailing side for the sole purpose of being eligible to move to reconsider.
2. Even if a member had failed to vote with the prevailing side, a vote could be changed just prior to the final announcement of the vote, making the member eligible to move reconsideration.
3. Except in case of a roll call it was impossible to determine accurately how anyone voted.
4. In a ballot vote, no one should be asked how he or she voted because the inquiry would violate the fundamental principle of secrecy in a ballot vote.[65]

Parliamentarians love to argue this point.[66] For all the talk about the temptation for misuse, we are amazed at how seriously delegates take the requirement of having voted on the prevailing side. When the chair asks, "Did you vote on the prevailing side?" one often hears "Oops, no," and the delegate runs around the convention floor to find someone who voted on the prevailing side. In our experience, the requirement has worked.

May a member who abstained or was not present for the vote move to reconsider?

No, not in the general meeting, where the motion may be made only by a member who voted on the prevailing side; but, yes, in committee. Anyone who did not vote on the losing side may make the motion (315, 329–30). (See later question on Reconsider in committees, pages 106–7.)

Must the seconder of the motion to Reconsider have voted on the prevailing side?

No, the seconding may be done by any member (320).

Is a motion to Reconsider the vote on an undebatable motion debatable?

No (320).

What is unique about the precedence of the motion to Reconsider?

The *making* of the motion has higher precedence than the *consideration* of the motion. The making of the motion has the highest precedence of all motions (except the archaic "Reconsider and Enter on the Minutes"), but the consideration of the motion has precedence only over any new main motion. Because the motion to Reconsider must be made during the same meeting and because the making of the motion temporarily suspends any action resulting from the vote it is proposing to reconsider, it is given such high precedence in terms of making the motion (78, 238, 317).

The uniqueness of the precedence can be confusing, but if someone interrupts pending business to move to reconsider a vote taken earlier in the meeting, the chair simply

1. asks, if there is any doubt, whether the maker voted on the prevailing side,

2. asks for a second,

3. has the secretary record that the motion to Reconsider is moved and seconded,

4. returns to the pending business, and

5. when pending business is disposed of, places the motion to Reconsider before the assembly and asks if there is any debate.

If the motion to Reconsider is made when no business is pending, the chair

1. asks, if there is any doubt, whether the maker voted on the prevailing side,

2. asks for a second, and

3. states, "It is moved and seconded to reconsider the vote on the motion to . . . The question is: shall the assembly reconsider the vote? Is there debate on the motion to Reconsider?"

After the vote on the original motion, how soon, how often, and for how long may a member make the motion to Reconsider?

How soon? A member may move to reconsider the vote on the original motion immediately.

How often? Ordinarily just once, but if the motion to Reconsider is voted on and lost, it can only be renewed by unanimous consent or, if the original motion was voted on and adopted, it was "materially amended" during its first reconsideration (321). An example of *materially amended* follows:

A motion to have a candidate forum Sunday afternoon is adopted.

A motion to Reconsider the vote on the motion to have a candidate forum is adopted.

The motion to have a candidate forum Sunday afternoon is amended by striking "forum" and inserting "debate."

The motion to have a candidate debate Sunday afternoon is adopted.

Is it in order to reconsider the vote on the motion to have a candidate debate Sunday afternoon? Yes, because it is not the same main motion that was reconsidered earlier.

For how long may a member make the motion to Reconsider? Until the end of the same meeting at which the vote on the original motion was taken.

Actually, *Robert's* says the same "day," not "meeting," and there is an exception: "In a convention or session of more than one day, a reconsideration can be moved only on the same day the original vote was taken or on the next succeeding day within the session on which a business meeting is held" (316).

Delegates to a convention should make note of the exception. In a three-day, Thursday, Friday, Saturday convention, action taken on Thursday may be reconsidered on Friday but not on Saturday.

The rule appears arbitrary, but there is a reason. Unlike organizations with weekly or monthly meetings, an organization with an annual convention must live for a full year with any mistakes. Unfortunately, delegates often are not as well prepared or as familiar with the issues or the procedures as they should be. As a result, mistakes are made that are often not realized until the day's—and evening's—work is completed. So, a motion to Reconsider is needed the next day. But to allow reconsideration on the third day runs the risk that a majority the first day (Thursday) could see their action overturned by an influx of delegates on the third day (Saturday).

Does the motion to Reconsider reopen the original motion to debate?

In effect, yes. Reconsider "is debatable in all cases in which the motion proposed to be reconsidered is debatable, and when debatable, opens to debate the merits of the question whose reconsideration is proposed" (320, 399). (Compare to "Postpone Indefinitely," page 21, and "Substitute," page 29.)

Is a motion to Reconsider the votes on several motions adopted or rejected earlier in order?

No, but this is where necessity meets rule, or principle. *Robert's* says that a motion to Reconsider enables a majority "to bring back for further consideration a [single] motion which has already been voted on" (315). Convention parliamentarians are aware, however, that the end of a convention sometimes finds a delegate moving "to reconsider the vote on all new business items and resolutions." The purpose of this motion, of course, is not to revisit earlier proposals, but to "clinch" them. That is, to make certain they will not be brought up again later (since the motion to Reconsider cannot be reconsidered).

If the motion to "Reconsider all business items" is a ceremonial end to the convention, there may be no harm. However, if the convention continues and the motion is intended to prohibit business from being revisited, beware. There are times that a convention must revisit business to correct an error or address an emergency. In addition, this mutated motion combines Suspend the Rules and Reconsider but is then voted on backwards by seeking a negative vote! If such a bloc motion to Reconsider is permitted, it should at least be treated as a motion to Suspend the Rules "to prohibit the reconsideration of any resolutions" and require a two-thirds vote.[67] However, the better course is to avoid the combined motion altogether, as the dangers outweigh the benefits.

What is the vote required for the motion to Reconsider?

Reconsider requires only a majority vote, "*regardless of the vote necessary to adopt the motion to be reconsidered*" (320). (For an exception, see later question on Reconsider in committees, page 107.)

May a vote to amend the bylaws be reconsidered?

If the motion to amend the bylaws was rejected, yes; if it was adopted, no. The rationale is based on the fact that such amendments require previous notice and become a part of the bylaws upon adoption. Thus, allowing reconsideration of an adopted amendment to the bylaws would allow a change to the bylaws without following the required procedures.[68]

What are the strategic uses of the motion to Reconsider?

There are two, each with its own rationale:

1. Because the motion to Reconsider may be made immediately following the vote on the original motion and may be made only once, those in the majority may move to reconsider while they are assured of retaining the majority. Later in the meeting, if tardy members should change the balance of power and they are able to persuade a member of the majority to move to reconsider the vote, the motion to Reconsider could not be used.

2. Because the motion to Reconsider is debatable and reopens the main motion to debate, it creates a situation that allows debate on a motion on which a vote has already been taken. For example, if the assembly votes to close debate on a main motion before a member has had a chance to present an argument, that member may vote on the prevailing side and then rise immediately after the vote is announced and move to reconsider the vote. If the motion is seconded, the member accomplishes her goal to debate the main motion even after the call for the Previous Question has been adopted and after the main motion was voted on.

Are the requirements for the motion to Reconsider different in committee?

Yes, there are four differences:

1. time limit (in committee, there is no limit);
2. the number of times the motion may be made (in committee, there is no limit to the number of times a question can be reconsidered);
3. who may make the motion (motion to Reconsider "can be made by any member of the committee who *did not vote with the losing side*;

or, in other words, the maker of the motion to *Reconsider* can be one who voted with the prevailing side, or one who did not vote at all, or even was absent" (330); and

4. the vote required ("Unless all the members of the committee who voted with the prevailing side are present or have been notified that the reconsideration will be moved, it requires a *two-thirds vote* to adopt the motion to *Reconsider*" (330).

Also, the motion to Reconsider cannot be used in committee of the whole (330). In a standing or special committee, the purpose is to work on a subject until "truth" has been found, so the opportunity for reconsideration is broadened. The purpose of a committee of the whole is simply to free the assembly from its restrictions on debate.

Reconsider and Enter on the Minutes

What is the purpose of the motion to Reconsider and Enter on the Minutes?

The purpose is "to prevent a temporary majority from taking advantage of an unrepresentative attendance at a meeting to vote an action that is opposed by a majority of a society's or a convention's membership" (332).

How is the purpose accomplished?

A member moves "to reconsider and enter on the minutes the vote on . . ." If a member seconds the motion, all action "required by the vote proposed to be considered is suspended" until the next meeting (335). In other words, the effect of making and seconding the motion is that of preventing final action on a main motion until another meeting of the organization on another day. The purpose, then, is to allow two members of an organization to protect the organization from itself.

How is the motion to Reconsider and Enter on the Minutes different from the motion to Reconsider?

First, it may be moved only on the same day on which the vote proposed to be reconsidered was taken. Reconsider may be moved on the following day if at a convention of more than one day.

Second, it takes precedence over the motion to Reconsider.

Third, it may be applied only to votes that finally dispose of main motions.

Fourth, it may not be applied to votes on motions whose object would be defeated by a delay of one day.

Fifth, in an organization that does not have regular business sessions as often as quarterly, it may not be moved at the last business meeting of the session.

Sixth, it may not be called up on the day it is made, except that, when it is moved on the last day—but not the last meeting—of a session of an organization having regular business sessions less often than quarterly, it can be called up at the last business meeting of the session (334).

If Reconsider is moved and lost, may a member move to reconsider and enter on the minutes?

No. It would not be in order to move to reconsider and enter on the minutes unless the motion is moved before the chair has announced the result of the vote on the motion to Reconsider (333).

Can the motion to Reconsider and Enter on the Minutes be misused?

Yes. Fortunately, the motion is almost never used. If it were used, it would place a difficult decision before the chair about whether the motion was being used properly. The idea that any two self-appointed members can save the organization from itself is rather difficult to swallow.[69] Those members who show up for meetings ought to be given the benefit of the doubt. Previous notice for the most important issues and agendas prepared in advance should be sufficient protection for absent members. At the meeting, using the regular motion to Reconsider or giving notice of intent to rescind ought to be sufficient. If it is not—which implies that the group cannot be trusted to take responsible action (especially after the opportunity for reconsideration)—the organization should adopt a higher (larger) quorum.

Motions That Bring a Question Again Before the Assembly

Motion	How Soon	How Often	How Long
Take from the Table	After some INTERVENING BUSINESS has been transacted	NO LIMIT as long as some further business has been transacted	If meet at least quarterly, then until the END OF FOLLOWING MEETING; or if meet less than quarterly, then until END OF SAME MEETING
Reconsider	IMMEDIATELY	ONCE unless if reconsidered and substantially amended or by unanimous consent	END OF SAME MEETING except in convention, END OF NEXT DAY
Rescind	IMMEDIATELY (BUT GENERALLY LATER MEETING) Rescind picks up where Reconsider leaves off	ONCE EACH MEETING	Theoretically FOREVER but cannot rescind action that cannot be undone

PART IV

Quorum

What is a quorum?

A quorum is the minimum number of members who must be present to conduct business (5, 21, 345).

Does a quorum refer to the number of members present or to the number voting?

A quorum always refers to the number of members present and not to the number voting (345).

How many members constitute a quorum?

Unless otherwise specified in the bylaws, the quorum for most meetings is a majority of the entire membership (21, 346).

How is a quorum determined for a convention?

In a body with delegates (convention, representative assembly, house of delegates), the quorum is "a majority of the number who have been registered as attending, irrespective of whether some may have departed. This may differ greatly from the number elected or appointed" (346). Remember the distinction: the number *registered*, not the number *elected*.

How may statutes affect quorum?

For many nonprofits, governmental bodies, homeowner and condominium associations, quorum is defined by statute. Be wary. Often such statutes define quorum differently or lead to results different from *Robert's*. For instance, it is not uncommon for statutes to provide that once a quorum is present, a quorum remains for the entire meeting regardless of how many members have left.[70]

Are vacancies taken into consideration in determining a quorum?

It depends. If quorum for a board is established in the bylaws as an absolute number, such as ten members, then vacancies make no difference. If, however, quorum is established as "a majority of the membership of the board," vacancies on the board will reduce the required quorum.[71]

What action may be taken in the absence of a quorum?

The only actions that may be taken in the absence of a quorum are to

1. Fix the Time to Which to Adjourn,
2. Adjourn,
3. Recess,
4. take measures to obtain a quorum (for example, move that absent members be contacted during a recess and asked to attend or that a call of the house be issued in assemblies having the power to compel attendance) (347–48, 350–51), and
5. according to the 11th Edition, certain subsidiary or incidental motions (such as to Raise a Question of Privilege) if related to "the conduct of the meeting while it remains without a quorum" (347–48).

Except for these procedural motions, any action taken in the absence of a quorum is "null and void." (347).

May a meeting without quorum be called to order?

Yes. "If a quorum cannot be obtained, the chair calls the meeting to order, announces the absence of a quorum, and entertains a motion to adjourn or one of the other motions allowed" (349).

What if the organization has important business that cannot be delayed and there is no quorum?

Robert's begins with a firm statement that no business can be conducted and then backs off, providing a loophole for emergency situations. In three consecutive sentences, *Robert's* states:

1. "The prohibition against transacting business in the absence of a quorum cannot be waived even by unanimous consent."
2. "If there is important business that should not be delayed until the next regular meeting, the assembly should fix the time for an adjourned meeting and then adjourn."
3. "If, instead, the members present take action informally in the absence of a quorum, they do so at their own risk" (348).

The third sentence can cover a multitude of sins, but the option must be available for actual emergencies. The risk is that the assembly may not later ratify the action taken.

Is the chair included in determining a quorum?

Yes, if the chair is a member.[72]

When the president is an ex officio member of a committee, is he or she included in the quorum?

No. "As an ex-officio member of a committee, the president has the same rights as the other committee members, but is not obligated to attend meetings of the committee and is not counted in determining the number required for a quorum or whether a quorum is present" (457, 497).

How does a member call to the attention of the chair that a quorum is no longer present?

The member rises to a Point of Order but may not interrupt a person who is speaking (349).

When business is transacted in a meeting where no one points out a quorum has been lost, is the business valid?

Yes, but here is the area in parliamentary procedure most susceptible to malfeasance and thus open to court action that questions an assumption of parliamentary law. Five steps are involved in revealing the rationale—and the problem:

1. The chair should stop the meeting when the quorum is lost. "If the chair notices the absence of a quorum, it is his duty to declare the fact" (349).

2. If the chair neglects or overlooks this responsibility, any member should make a Point of Order that the quorum has been lost.

3. If the chair rules the Point of Order not well taken, a member may Appeal from the decision of the chair.

4. Since parliamentary procedure is grounded in the premise of good faith—that the chair is honest and that the members will correct errors of the chair—"the continued presence of a quorum is presumed" (349). Because of the presumption of good faith and the "difficulty likely

to be encountered in determining exactly how long the meeting has been without a quorum in such cases," the general rule is that "a point of order relating to the absence of a quorum is generally not permitted to affect prior action" (349).

But what happens if the chair does not notice the lack of a quorum and rules that a member's Point of Order of no quorum is not well taken and the members sustain the decision of the chair? The answer is a fifth step in determining whether a quorum is present. If this happens, the chair's intent may not be malevolent. Take, for example, a three-day convention consisting of one thousand delegates. Delegates are told on Thursday that they may submit motions (new business items) that will be considered on Saturday. On Saturday, the budget is adopted, the dues are established, and, exhausted from dealing with the big issues, many delegates leave and the quorum is lost. The chair faces a dilemma; he should follow the rules, but he also wants "to be fair" to those members who have waited so long for their voices to be heard. If the chair rules no quorum, these delegates head home feeling betrayed.

5. When the presumption of a quorum has clearly been abused, the presumption can be challenged even after the fact. Upon "clear and convincing proof," a Point of Order "can be given effect retrospectively by a ruling of the presiding officer, subject to appeal" (349). Such instances are rare. After all, the number of members voting on an issue will not impact quorum, as some members may have abstained. But if the number of members present can somehow be established after the fact (e.g., there was a roll-call), the lack of quorum can be challenged at any time.[73] In general then, after adjournment, it is too late to question a quorum.

Does a gathering with no quorum count as a meeting?

Robert's provides that even if a meeting lacks quorum, any requirement that the meeting be held has been complied with even though no business can be conducted (347).

Meetings

Should our organization follow *Robert's*?

Most organizations are not required to have a parliamentary authority, but many procedural problems can be avoided by designating one. For organizations with a parliamentary authority, *Robert's* is by far the most popular choice. Typically, a parliamentary authority is established in the governing documents, such as bylaws or convention rules. For some types of organizations—governmental bodies, homeowner associations, condominium associations—a parliamentary authority may be prescribed by statute.[74] An organization with no parliamentary authority can adopt one through a two-thirds vote (15–17).

May we hold electronic meetings, such as by telephone or videoconference?

The 11th Edition expands coverage of electronic meetings but emphasizes that "simultaneous aural communication" is an essential element of a meeting (98). If a board or committee is established in the bylaws, only a bylaws provision can authorize valid electronic meetings (98). The 11th Edition includes a number of suggested rules on the conduct of electronic meetings (99). As a caveat, many state statutes regulate when and how boards can meet by telephone. *Robert's* notes elsewhere that obtaining separate telephone approval from each board member individually is not official action, as it was not taken at a single meeting where the members could "mutually debate and decide the matter as a deliberative body" (487).

What are the differences between the types of business meetings?

A *regular meeting* is the recurring business meeting of an organization at regular intervals (89). A *special meeting* is a meeting held at a time other than a regular meeting to consider specific items noticed in the call of the meeting. Provision for a special meeting must be in an organization's bylaws, or (according to the 11th Edition), a part of a disciplinary proceeding (90–92). An *adjourned meeting* is a continuation of a prior meeting for purposes of resuming work where it was interrupted (93). (*The Standard Code* more descriptively calls this a *continued* meeting.) Depending on the type of organization, an *annual meeting* can either be the once-a-year meeting of the members or a designated regular meeting at which certain actions are taken, such as the election of officers (94).

What is an executive session?

An executive session is a meeting or portion of meeting in which the proceedings are secret (95). Only members (i.e., board members for a board meeting, members for a membership meeting) are permitted to remain for an executive session; although certain nonmembers are sometimes invited to remain, such as the attorney or parliamentarian. Even minutes of an executive session are only acted upon in executive session (96). Previously, *Robert's* provided that "in most organizations . . . board or committee meetings are customarily held in executive session." That language has been removed, and the 11th Edition simply states: "A meeting enters into executive session only when required by rule or established custom, or upon the adoption of a motion to do so" (95). For organizations governed by statute—city councils, county commissions, legislative bodies, homeowner associations, condominiums—the right and method for going into executive session is often mandated by law.

How does a public session differ from a regular meeting?

For governmental bodies subject to "sunshine laws," most meetings must be held within public view (96). Because of governing documents or laws, members of the public may have the right to attend meetings or to address the group. Generally, though, such nonmembers have no right to debate issues, make motions, or object to unanimous consent.

How may an item be delayed from one meeting to another?

For groups that meet at least quarterly, business can be carried over to the next meeting by:

1. postponing to a certain time;
2. laying on the table;
3. "going over to the later session as unfinished business or as an unfinished special order";

4. making the motion to Reconsider, but not calling it up, at the current meeting; and

5. referring to committee. (90–91)

While item 3 is new to the 11th Edition, it recognizes the existing rule that an item pending or not yet reached on the order of business is carried over to the next session (236–37).

What is the difference between a meeting and a session?

A meeting "is a single official gathering . . . in one room or area to transact business for a length of time during which there is no cessation of proceedings and the members do not separate, unless for a short recess" (81–82). (Think: school board, local union, city council, student government *meeting*.) A session "is a meeting or series of connected meetings devoted to a single order of business, program, agenda, or announced purpose, in which—when there is more than one meeting—each succeeding meeting is scheduled with a view to continuing business at the point where it was left off at the previous meeting" (2, 82, 601). (Think: convention with several meetings is the *annual session*.)

Conventions

How is a convention brought to order?

The official organization of a convention is brought about by the adoption of the reports of three committees: "the Credentials Committee, the Committee on Standing Rules, and the Program Committee, in that order" (609–10). "Before the Credentials Committee report is adopted, since the membership has not been established, the only motions that are in order are those related to its consideration or to the conduct of the meeting before its adoption, as well as those that are in order in the absence of a quorum" (615).[75]

In a convention, what rules apply before adoption of the standing rules?

In the 10th edition, while unstated, the answer would necessarily be that the rules in the parliamentary authority would apply. The 11th Edition eliminates any confusion by stating: "Until the proposed standing rules are adopted, the convention is governed by the rules in the organization's parliamentary authority, such as those concerning the seating of delegates and alternates and assignment of the floor" (618).

At a convention, may a member who is not a delegate participate in debate?

No, not unless given permission by the body or a specific rule. Usually, courtesy is extended to the member by the chair asking for unanimous consent to allow the member to speak. If there is objection, a majority vote is required to allow the nondelegate to speak.

May an item be carried over or postponed from one convention to another?

Generally, no. If a group meets less often than quarterly, business can only go over to the next meeting by being referred to a committee (90–91). (See "Postpone to a Certain Time (or Definitely)," pages 45–46.)

Boards

What rules of procedure should a board use?

Robert's outlines very relaxed procedures for boards "where there are not more than about a dozen members present," including:

1. "Members may raise a hand instead of standing when seeking to obtain the floor, and may remain seated while making motions or speaking" (487).

2. Motions need no second.

3. Discussion of a subject is permitted while no motion is pending.

4. When a proposal is clear, a vote can be taken without a formal motion.

5. There is no limit to the number of times a member may speak to a subject or motion. While motions for the Previous Question or to Limit or Extend Limits of Debate are in order, "occasions where they are necessary or appropriate may be rarer than in larger assemblies" (488).

6. The chair may participate in debate, make motions, and vote.

7. Votes can initially be taken by a show of hands (487–89).

In contrast, large boards follow formal procedures.

What are the rights of an ex officio member of a board?

If a person is a member of the organization, there is no distinction between ex officio and regular membership. If a person is not a member of the organization, an ex officio member has all of the privileges but none of the obligations of membership and is not counted in determining a quorum (483–84).

May a board meet by telephone?

Robert's provides that boards "can transact business only in a regular or properly called meeting of which every board member has been notified" and a quorum is present (486–87). The 11th Edition expands coverage of certain electronic meetings—whether by telephone or Internet—if authorized in the bylaws and "so long as the meetings provide, at a minimum, conditions of opportunity for simultaneous aural communication among all participating members equivalent to those of meetings held in one room or area" (97). Certain other rules may be advisable if electronic meetings are authorized (98–99).

Minutes

What should go in the minutes of a meeting?

Minutes are a record of action taken at the meeting, *not* what was said by members or guests. So, unless a statute or rule requires more, minutes take the following form:

First Paragraph:
   Kind of meeting (regular, special, adjourned)
   Name of organization
   Date and time of meeting
   Place of meeting, if it varies
   Presence of chair and secretary, or if absent, name of substitute
   Whether minutes of previous meeting were read and approved

Separate paragraph for each subject matter with name of mover:
   All main motions or motions to bring a main question again before
      the assembly

(except any withdrawn) stating:

> the wording in which adopted or disposed of;
>
> the disposition of motion (including amendments or secondary motions);
>
> number of votes if count ordered or ballot vote;
>
> names and votes if roll-call vote;
>
> all notices of motion; and
>
> all Points of Order and Appeals, whether sustained or lost.

Last Paragraph:

> Hour of adjournment. (468–71)

Should the names of makers and seconders of motions be included in the minutes?

According to *Robert's*, the names of makers of main motions should be entered in the minutes; there is no need to list seconders' names (470).

Can minutes be prepared before the meeting?

Model minutes or "skeletal minutes" are draft minutes prepared in advance of a meeting that include "everything that will occur, in the order it will occur, based on the agenda and the script for the meeting."[76] At the meeting, only details such as which motions were adopted or lost must be completed. Through this method, even the minutes of a multiday convention can be quickly completed immediately following the meeting.

Must minutes be read aloud at a meeting?

The older practice of reading minutes aloud is no longer necessary if the minutes have been sent to members in advance, unless a member requests that they be read (354).

Should annual meetings approve minutes?

No. In organizations that meet yearly, such as the annual meeting of a community association or a convention, members are unlikely to recall what happened a year earlier. In fact, the voting body may be composed of completely different members. Because of this, *Robert's* advises that minutes "of one annual meeting should not be held for action until the next one a year later" (95). Instead, "the executive board or a committee appointed for the purpose should be authorized to approve the minutes" (474–75).

What is the simplest method for approving minutes?

By unanimous consent. Much time can be saved by the chair simply asking, "Are there any corrections to the minutes?" (354). After any corrections are resolved, the chair asks, "Is there objection to approving the minutes? Hearing no objection, the minutes are approved."[77] If a member objects, the chair can proceed with obtaining a motion to approve the minutes.

How are minutes of an executive session handled?

Because minutes are a record of what was done at a meeting, and not what was said, there may be little in the way of minutes from a closed meeting consisting of discussion. If action was taken, there would be minutes, but such a record would only be available to those who had a right to be in the executive session and would need to be approved later at a meeting held in executive session (96).

Must minutes be signed "Respectfully submitted"?

No, that is an older practice that is no longer followed (471).

Voting

How is majority vote defined?

Unless defined differently in the bylaws, a majority vote is *more than half of the votes cast* (54, 400).

Three features are important here:

1. The definition is *more than half—not* "one more than half." What can happen if the definition is one more than half?

> CHAIR: By a vote of thirteen to twelve, the motion is adopted.
> MEMBER: Madam Chairman, what was that vote again?
> CHAIR: Thirteen to twelve.
> MEMBER: How many votes were cast?
> CHAIR: Twenty-five.
> MEMBER: How do we define majority?
> CHAIR: One more than half.
> MEMBER: What is half of twenty-five?
> CHAIR: Twelve and one-half.
> MEMBER: What is one more than half?
> CHAIR: Thirteen and one-half.
> MEMBER: What was that vote again?
> CHAIR: Oops.

The same problem occurs if majority is incorrectly defined as 51 percent. Again, majority means more than half, *not* 51 percent, *not* one more than half. *Do not make this mistake!* This can be the result:If Thomas Laehn . . . would have received half a vote more in the student government election, he would have been named Drake University's 2002–2003 student body president on Tuesday night. However, as it stands, an online runoff election will take place on Monday, Feb. 25, from 11 A.M. to 4:30 P.M. between Laehn and Erika Grimwood. . . .

The rules of student government elections state that a candidate "must receive one-half of the votes plus one vote" to win the race. In a presidential race where 741 students voted, Laehn received 371 votes, Grimwood received 320 votes, and David Norber . . . received 50 votes.[78]

Although 371 is a majority ("more than half") of 741, no one was elected in this situation because of a rule redefining a majority as "half plus one." The moral? Parliamentary procedure is complicated and difficult enough as it is; do not create unnecessary problems.

2. The definition is *votes cast*: not votes of members present; not votes of the membership; not votes of the members in good standing. The point is that only those who engage in the act of voting (either for or against) determine whether a motion is adopted.

For example, an organization has one hundred members. Eighty are present at a meeting. On a main motion, fifty members vote. How many members must vote in favor of the motion for it to pass? Answer: twenty-six. At the same meeting, a motion could be adopted by a vote of one in favor and none opposed.

3. The definition is *all votes. Robert's* says "more than half of the votes cast by persons entitled to vote, excluding blanks or abstentions" (400). That means, if a voter entitled to vote casts an illegal vote, the vote counts toward the number voting. Again, *Robert's*: "All ballots that indicate a preference—provided they have been cast by persons entitled to vote—are taken into account in determining the number of votes cast for purposes of computing the majority" (415).[79]

How can a two-thirds vote be quickly calculated?

If you are without electronics, *Demeter's Manual* suggests applying this simple formula: "*Double* the number of votes cast for the *negative* side; if the negative votes exceed (are more than) the number of votes cast for the affirmative side, you do not have a 2/3 vote."[80]

May the usual bases for determining a majority or two-thirds vote be changed?

Yes. Specific bylaws language or state statutes may sometimes change votes from being based on those members "present and voting" to some other denominator, such as the percentage of "members present" or "the entire membership."

What is an illegal vote?

An illegal vote is, of course, a vote that is not legal. A vote is illegal if two completed ballots are folded together (both are rejected and count as one vote cast); if the vote is for too many candidates; if the vote is unintelligible; if the vote is for an unidentifiable candidate; or if the vote is for a fictional character (415–17). The illegal vote in each case is included in the number of votes cast.

A distinction must be made between an illegal vote made by a member entitled to vote and a vote made by a person not entitled to vote. Any vote by a person who is not entitled to vote is an illegal vote, and the vote is not included in the number of votes cast. If it appears that ballots cast by persons not entitled to vote might have affected the result, a new ballot must be taken (416).

A blank ballot is not a vote; it is a blank, and it is not counted in the number of votes cast.

The Standard Code avoids the confusion and potential problems over illegal votes by defining majority vote as more than half of the legal votes cast, meaning that both blank and illegal ballots are ignored.[81]

Are abstentions counted in the vote?

No (45, 400, 403, 407), unless some rule requires that the vote be based on a percentage of the "total membership," in which case everyone who doesn't vote in favor is counted the same as a "no" vote.

Should the chair call for abstentions?

No (45).

What is a "simple majority" or "two-thirds majority"?

Poor wording. "Majority" means "more than half" (400). "Two-thirds" means "at least two thirds" (401). Other words are unnecessary and confusing.[82]

Can a member be prevented from voting when others feel the member has a personal or financial interest in the question to be decided?

No. This can be a trying situation. *Robert's* states that "No member should vote on a question in which he has a direct personal or pecuniary interest" (407). (An exception is made when others are included in the motion, such as a motion to hold a banquet or to discipline certain members). However, this prohibition on voting is for the member to claim. "No member can be compelled to refrain from voting in such circumstances" (407). (See "Getting Started," page 10.)

May the maker of a motion vote against his or her motion?

Yes, but the maker cannot speak against it (393). (See "Getting Started," page 10.)

What about a tie vote?

A motion either obtains a majority (or two-thirds) vote or it does not (53–54, 405–6). Since a majority vote is more than half the votes cast, a tie vote simply means that the motion is rejected. When the vote results in a tie, the chair should state, "By a vote of ten in favor and ten against, the motion is lost. The next item of business is . . ." (See next question if the chair intends to vote). Members who recall the times when they used to hem and haw over what to do about a tie vote will be in awe of the chair's efficiency and knowledge of parliamentary procedure.

When may the chair vote?

Theoretically, the presiding officer has the same voting privileges as every other member. In practice, however, the chair's adherence to this privilege when the vote is by voice or by show of hands would conflict with the responsibility to remain impartial. *Robert's* recognizes the right of the chair to vote, but suggests that the chair protect impartiality by "exercising his voting right only when the vote would affect the outcome" (50, 53–54, 405–6). Thus, the chair may vote to break a tie in favor of a motion she favors or to create a tie if against a motion. The reverse is also true: when the vote is a tie or a motion is adopted by one vote, the chair affects the result by *not* voting. If the chair is against the motion and the vote is a tie, the chair is in effect voting against the motion by declining to vote in favor. If the motion is adopted by one vote, the chair is in effect voting for the motion by declining to vote.

A statement that the chair can vote to break a tie is half wrong and therefore misleading. The expression *break a tie* should be replaced with the phrase *affect the outcome*. The principle applies equally to decisions requiring a two-thirds vote.

May the chair vote twice, once as a member and once as the chair?

No (406).

How is plurality vote defined?

A plurality vote is "the largest number of votes to be given any candidate or proposition when three or more choices are possible; the candidate or proposition receiving the largest number of votes has a plurality" (404–5). The definition means that a plurality *may* be a majority, but usually the connotation of plurality is that the candidate or proposition has more votes than any other candidate or proposition, but not a majority.

Does a plurality elect?

No. Unless the bylaws provide for election by plurality, a majority vote is required to elect a candidate or to adopt a motion (405). It should be noted that in the nonprofit world, statutes often provide that directors are elected by a plurality vote.[83]

Should a two-thirds vote be required on matters for which broad support of the members is needed (such as adoption of dues)?

Absolutely not. Many people mistakenly reason that if majority support is good, two-thirds support is better; therefore, an organization should require a two-thirds vote for its most controversial issues. The mistake is in the leap from wanting broad support to requiring a two-thirds vote. Requiring a two-thirds vote produces exactly the opposite effect. Any decision requiring a two-thirds vote turns over control to a minority of one-third plus one. *The Standard Code* says it best:

> Some people mistakenly assume that the higher the vote required to take an action, the greater the protection of the members. Instead, the opposite is true. Whenever a vote of more than a majority is required to take an action, control is taken from the majority and given to a minority. For example, when a two-thirds vote is required, the minority need be only one-third plus one member to defeat the proposal. Thus, a minority is permitted to overrule the will, not only of the majority, but of almost two-thirds of the members.[84]

Take, for example, an organization that requires a majority vote to adopt the budget and a two-thirds vote to adopt the dues (such organizations exist). The budget is adopted by a vote of 650 in favor to 350 against; it has overwhelming support. The assembly turns to the motion to set the dues at a figure reflecting the budget. The vote is 650 in favor; 350 against. The motion is rejected. Rather than create broad support for the dues, the requirement of a two-thirds vote has created 650 delegates who are outraged at being held hostage by a minority. Some consensus. More than once we have seen it happen. It is not pretty.[85]

Concerning budgets and dues, is a motion in order to assess members for payments beyond the dues?

No, not unless it is provided for in the bylaws (572). Most organizations do not have such a standing provision, so a proposal to assess members would need to be accompanied by or in the form of a motion to amend the bylaws. (See "Bylaws," page 140.)

May votes be taken or decisions made online, by e-mail or fax?

Not typically. "A group that attempts to conduct the deliberative process in writing (such as by postal mail, e-mail, 'chat rooms,' or fax)—which is not recommended—does not constitute a deliberative assembly. Any such effort may achieve a consultative character, but it is foreign to the deliberative process as understood under parliamentary law" (98). "When making decisions by such means, many situations unprecedented in parliamentary law will arise, and many of its rules and customs will not be applicable" (1).[86] Interestingly, the 11th Edition adds the comment that "the personal approval of a proposed action obtained . . . in writing, even from every member of the board, is not the approval of the board" (487). Many state statutes provide that nonprofit boards can make decisions by unanimous written consent, but that is a statutory provision and not due to *Robert's*.

Should an organization allow straw polls?

No. A straw vote is more than an innocent effort to get a sense of where members stand on a question; it can be used to mislead members. *Robert's* comes down hard on straw voting: "STRAW POLLS NOT IN ORDER. A motion to take an informal straw poll to 'test the water' is not in order because it neither adopts nor rejects a measure and hence is meaningless and dilatory" (429). One strategic purpose of the motion to Postpone Indefinitely is to provide a straw poll on the main motion, which is why some parliamentary authorities criticize the motion.[87] (See "Postpone Indefinitely," page 21.)

May a member change his or her vote?

Until the vote is announced, yes (48). After the vote is announced, a request to change one's vote must be made "immediately after the chair's announcement, before any debate or business has intervened" (409). The request is undebatable and requires the unanimous consent of the body (408).

This distinction extends to a vote by mail. If the ballot is identifiable and if the request is submitted before the deadline for receiving votes, a member may change her vote.[88]

May a member vote by proxy?

Not unless authorized in the bylaws (423–24, 428–29) or provided by state law.

May a member interrupt a vote, such as raising a Point of Order, a Parliamentary Inquiry, or a Question of Privilege?

No. "Interruptions during the taking of a vote are permitted only before any member has actually voted, unless, as sometimes occurs in ballot voting, other business is being transacted during voting or tabulating" (408, 250–51).[89] The 11th Edition makes clear that a Point of Order regarding the conduct of the vote must be raised immediately following the announcement of the vote and "before any debate or business has intervened" (250–51, 408–9).

The chair must do two things prior to any vote:

1. Clearly, concisely, and carefully state the question on the vote about to be taken. Particularly on controversial matters, the chair must make every reasonable effort to ensure that delegates are paying attention and understand the consequences of the action they are about to take.

2. Take the vote *without interruption*. To allow the vote to be interrupted is to ask for trouble, in that it could affect the vote of members who have not yet voted.

May a member explain his or her vote during the vote?

No, explaining means debating (408).

Who may vote when a counted vote is taken a second time?

If a vote is taken a second time, the same rules apply that were in effect for the first vote. In other words, if a member voted and then left, the member has lost the right to vote; if a member arrives after the first vote, he is entitled to vote on the second vote.

This situation occurs at conventions, and delegates are at first confused and then furious when they are informed of the rule. Delegates must understand that, if they neglect their responsibility to remain at the convention, they forfeit their right to vote. The delegate is elected to conduct the business of the organization. If an unfortunate error should occur, requiring a second vote, ensuring an accurate vote (e.g., election) is part of the business of the convention; and in the process, members may switch their votes.[90]

Who decides the method and procedure for voting?

Unless the bylaws provide otherwise, the assembly decides (409).

What is a roll-call vote?

A roll-call vote forces members on record as to their positions. Typically, the roll is called in alphabetical order and one by one all the members announce their vote by stating *aye* (or "yes" or "yea"), *no* (or "nay"), or answers *present* (420). In conventions representing constituents, a rule may also permit a roll call to change the method of voting from one-person-one-vote to a weighted system where the membership represented is taken into account.

What is the vote required to have a roll-call vote?

A motion to vote by roll call requires a majority vote without debate. Conventions often—and should—have a rule that permits a minority (such as 1/3 or 1/5) to demand a roll call. When such a rule exists, the chair states: "There is a request for a roll-call vote. Those in favor of taking a roll-call vote, please stand. Seeing more than/fewer than one-third of the members present standing, we will/will not have a roll-call vote." Without such a rule, a motion for a roll call requires a majority vote, and it is unlikely that the majority will vote to require the majority to go on record.

May the assembly go from a voice vote to a ballot vote?

Yes, unless the bylaws provide otherwise, the assembly decides without debate and by majority vote (412–13).

May the assembly go from a ballot vote, as required in the bylaws, to a voice vote?

No. If the bylaws require that the vote be taken by ballot, no method of voting is in order that forces the disclosure of a member's vote (263, 412–13, 441–42, 573).

Must the chair always call for the negative vote?

Yes, "except that this rule is commonly relaxed in the case of noncontroversial motions of a complimentary or courtesy nature" (xxxiv, 45). Other than this exception, for both procedural and fairness reasons, the negative vote should always be taken.[91]

How does the chair ask for unanimous consent?

When members universally favor a proposal or on less significant matters, a chair may simply ask if there is opposition to a motion, rather than taking a formal vote. According to *Robert's* in such instances, the chair asks, "If there is no objection to . . ." or "Is there any objection to . . . ?" (54–56). ("Is there objection to . . . ?" seems clearer). Without objection, the motion is adopted. If a member objects, the chair states the question on the motion and takes a formal vote (54). (See "Amend (the Amending Process)," page 26, "Previous Question (Close Debate)," page 57, and "Modify or Withdraw a Motion," pages 96–97, for examples where the chair may ask for unanimous consent.)

May a vote that was not unanimous be made unanimous by moving that the vote be made unanimous?

No, in nearly all cases. With respect to votes taken by voice, by show of hands, by standing, or by roll call, the answer is no.

With respect to votes taken by ballot, the answer is no unless the motion to make a ballot vote unanimous is also voted on by ballot (413).

It is common practice at political conventions to vote to make a nomination unanimous. The purpose is to give the appearance of unity, but it is not a proper motion.

What is a consent calendar?

A *consent calendar* or *consent agenda* is used by some organizations, particularly governmental bodies, to quickly move through routine matters (361). While the exact process of consent calendars vary and should be established by a special rule of order, a typical practice is to place the consent calendar near the start of the meeting and include all noncontroversial items, such as adoption of the minutes. Any member may request that an item be removed and placed on the regular agenda for consideration and vote. The remaining consent-calendar items are then unanimously approved as a unit without discussion.

What is cumulative voting?

In cumulative voting, a member has as many votes as the number of options being voted on. For instance, if there are five board members being elected, each member can cast up to five votes. The member can cast up to one vote for five different candidates or cast five votes for one candidate. Cumulative voting is rare, often seen only in voting by corporations, and must be authorized by the bylaws or statute (443–44).[92]

What is preferential voting?

Preferential voting is any number of methods by which members can rank their votes on a single ballot when there are multiple choices (425–28). Repeated balloting is unnecessary, in that the voter states a preference as to first choice, second choice, etc. The types of preferential voting are legion (with such names as "Single Transferable Vote" or "Single Transferable Vote with Quota"). In some methods, the lowest vote getters are quickly eliminated. In others, votes are reassigned until one candidate receives a majority.[93]

Nominations and Elections

Must a member be nominated before he or she can be elected?

No. Nominations simply serve the practical purpose of informing members of which individuals are interested in running and thus expedite the business of the assembly (430–31). The 11th Edition adds the observation that "Without nominations, voting might have to be repeated many times before a candidate achieved the required majority" (431).

Who decides nomination and election procedures?

As with voting procedures, unless specified in the bylaws, the body decides the procedures for nominations and elections (431, 438).

Most organizations that conduct elections at conventions specify election procedures in their bylaws or convention rules. If not, the chair should not use the assembly's right as an excuse not to lead. The more complete answer is that the chair, guided by the organization's rules and customs, should establish and present, subject to the assembly's approval, the procedures for nominations and elections.

Do nominations require a second?

No, but in many organizations it is customary to allow members to second a nomination to indicate endorsement (432).

Is it necessary to move to close nominations?

No, in fact, it is a waste of time. The chair should give ample time for nominations, ask, "Are there further nominations?" and, there being none, declare that nominations are closed (436).

What is the vote required to close nominations?

Two-thirds (288, 436).

What is the vote required to reopen nominations?

Majority (289, 436).

May members of the nominating committee be nominated?

Yes. If not, election to the nominating committee could be used to prevent a member from becoming a nominee (433). If the president has the authority to appoint the members, the problem can be avoided by appointing members to the committee who have expressed no interest in running for office.

May the nominating ballot be the electing ballot?

No. If the organization's bylaws require elections to be held by ballot, the vote must be by ballot (437). (See "Voting," page 132.)

If there is only one nominee for an office, may the chair declare the nominee the winner?

Not if the bylaws require that the vote be taken by ballot. On this point, it is not at all unusual for organizations to ignore their bylaws, but to do so deprives members of the privilege of voting for write-in candidates (443, 573). *Demeter's Manual* is music to the ears of those who ignore the rule: "If the bylaws specify that election shall be by roll call or secret ballot, and a vote on one or more unopposed candidates is taken by unanimous acclamation and thunderous applause instead, such an election is legal if no one objects."[94]

(For an explanation of why such a bylaws provision should not be ignored, see "Suspend the Rules," page 78, and "Voting," page 132.)

What about a tie vote in an election?

Unlike the vote on a motion (where a tie vote defeats the motion), a tie vote in an election where only one person is to be elected means that voting must continue. "If any office remains unfilled after the first ballot, as may happen if there are more than two nominees, the balloting is repeated for that office as many times as necessary to obtain a majority vote for a single candidate" (441).

If no one is elected, should the nominee receiving the lowest number of votes be removed from the next ballot?

No, although it is common practice. "When repeated balloting for an office is necessary, individuals are never removed from candidacy on the next ballot unless they voluntarily withdraw—which they are not obligated to do. The candidate in lowest place may turn out to be a 'dark horse' on whom all factions may prefer to agree" (441).

The 11th Edition includes a footnote that a special rule of order or a motion to Suspend the Rules could be used to remove the lowest vote-getter from succeeding ballots; but that only a bylaws provision could make a dropped nominee ineligible for election (441).

If more candidates receive a majority vote than positions open (as in electing a board), how is the result determined?

"If more than the prescribed number receive a majority vote, the places are filled by the proper number receiving the largest number of votes" (441).

Is an election null and void if there are illegal votes?

Under *Robert's*, an illegal vote cast by a voter entitled to vote is included in the number of votes cast. The illegal vote may affect the outcome; it does not nullify the election. For example, one hundred votes are cast for the office of president. Candidate Adams receives fifty votes; candidate Nelson receives forty-nine votes; one vote is illegal due to being unreadable. Candidate Adams is not elected. Fifty votes out of one hundred votes cast is not more than half of the votes cast.

A situation can arise where votes cast by persons who are not entitled to vote can nullify an election:

> The principle followed is that a choice has no mandate from the voting body unless approval is expressed by more than half of those entitled to vote and registering any evidence of having some preference. . . . If there is evidence that any unidentifiable ballots were cast by persons not entitled to vote, and if there is any possibility that such ballots might affect the result, the entire ballot is null and void, and a new ballot must be taken. (415–16)

Should the votes received be announced as part of the election results?

Always. Announcing the votes received by each candidate has procedural and political benefits. By hearing actual numbers, members may realize a counting or procedural error occurred in the balloting, which can then be corrected. In addition, candidates not elected may be less enthusiastic about challenging the results when they realize the vote spread was quite large. *Robert's* advises that the "tellers' report is entered in full in the minutes, becoming a part of the official record of the organization. Under no circumstances should this be omitted in an election or in a vote on a critical motion out of a mistaken deference to the feelings of unsuccessful candidates or members of the losing side" (418).

What is an election by acclamation?

In prior *Robert's*, the term *acclamation* signified a request that an election be held by unanimous consent. The 11th Edition makes this option the default by noting that if only one person is nominated and the bylaws do not require a ballot vote, the chair "simply declares that the nominee is elected, thus effecting the election by unanimous consent or 'acclamation'" (443).

Bylaws

How does an organization resolve a dispute when its rules are in conflict?

When rules of the same rank appear to be in conflict, a specific rule applies over a general rule (589).

How does an organization resolve a dispute over the meaning of its bylaws?

The best and most valuable guidelines were from *Parliamentary Law*, which were included for the first time in slightly modified language in the 1990 *Robert's* and still appear in the 11th Edition as "Some Principles of Interpretation":

> 1. *Each society decides for itself the meaning of its bylaws.* When the meaning is clear, however, the society, even by a unanimous vote, cannot change that meaning except by amending its bylaws. . . .
>
> 2. *When a provision of the bylaws is susceptible to two meanings, one of which conflicts with or renders absurd another bylaw provision, and the other meaning does not, the latter must be taken as the true meaning.* . . .
>
> 3. *A general statement or rule is always of less authority than a specific statement or rule and yields to it.* . . .
>
> 4. *If the bylaws authorize certain things specifically, other things of the same class are thereby prohibited.* . . .
>
> 5. *A provision granting certain privileges carries with it a right to a part of the privileges, but prohibits a greater privilege.* . . .
>
> 6. *A prohibition or limitation prohibits everything greater than what is prohibited, or that goes beyond the limitation; but it permits what is less than the limitation; and also permits things of the same class that are not mentioned in the prohibition or limitation and that are evidently not improper.* . . .

7. *The imposition of a definite penalty for a particular action prohibits the increase or diminution of the penalty. . . .*

8. *In cases where the bylaws use a general term and also two or more specific terms that are wholly included under the general one, a rule in which only the general term is used applies to all the specific terms.* (588–91)

What is the proper ruling when a custom and a rule are in conflict?

If not handled carefully, this is another situation that the chair cannot win. Take the example of amending bylaws. Some organizations misinterpret the requirement of previous notice to mean that motions to amend the motion to amend the bylaws are out of order. Thus, for years the organization has voted to adopt or reject amendments without allowing appropriate amendments from the floor. What does the chair do when a member raises a Point of Order that it is in order to amend amendments to the bylaws? If the chair rules that amendments are *not* in order, the chair is not adhering to the adopted rules of the society. If the chair rules that amendments *are* in order, he suffers the wrath of those who accuse young whippersnappers of trying to change the way things have always been done. To resolve the problem, the chair might state:

> The chair recognizes our custom has been to not allow floor amendments to proposed bylaws amendments. However, our parliamentary authority provides that if a custom or practice is in conflict with the parliamentary authority or any written rule, and a Point of Order is raised, the custom falls to the ground and the rule must be complied with unless changed (19). This Point of Order questions whether bylaws amendments can be amended from the floor. *Robert's Rules of Order Newly Revised*, pages 594–596, provides that they can so long as the amendment is within the scope of notice. As a result, the chair rules the Point of Order well taken. Primary and secondary amendments within the scope of notice will be permitted on proposed bylaws amendments.

A paragraph in the 11th Edition makes clear that custom bows to rule.

> In some organizations, a particular practice may sometimes come to be followed as a matter of established custom so that

it is treated practically as if it were prescribed by a rule. . . . However, if a customary practice is or becomes in conflict with the parliamentary authority or any written rule, and a *Point of Order* citing the conflict is raised at any time, the custom falls to the ground, and the conflicting provision in the parliamentary authority or written rule must thereafter be complied with. (19)

Case closed, and the Point of Order provided the opportunity to educate members about the misunderstanding of the requirement of notice and why their custom undermined the deliberative process.[95] (See "Amend (the Amending Process)," page 27.)

In a financial emergency, may members be assessed for payment in addition to dues?

No, not unless the bylaws provide for an assessment: "Members cannot be assessed any additional payment aside from their dues unless it is provided for in the bylaws" (572). In the absence of such a provision, a motion to assess members must be accompanied by a motion to amend the bylaws, and of course, the amendment is subject to any notice requirement to amend the bylaws. (See "Amend (the Amending Process)," page 27, and "Voting," page 129.)

If proposed amendments to the bylaws containing typographical errors are sent to members, and the errors are not discovered until after the deadline for notice, may those amendments be considered?

Yes, but obviously, the decision must be made with caution. The key is whether members understand the amendment. If there is doubt, the motion(s) should be ruled out of order.[96]

Can typographical corrections or changes to headings be made following the adoption of a bylaws amendment?

"Indisputably necessary changes in designation by number or letter may be presumed to have been included in the assembly's action even if they were not mentioned. . . . Only the assembly can amend captions or headings under the rules applicable to bylaws or other papers if such change could have any effect on meaning, and this authority may not be delegated" (598).

When do adopted bylaw amendments go into effect?

Immediately, unless the motion to adopt specifies another time for the amendment to become effective (597). Some organizations have a bylaws provision as to when bylaw amendments go into effect. Without such a provision, there are two ways to specify a time for the amendment to go into effect:

1. A motion to Amend can be made to add a clause, such as "with the proviso that this amendment shall not go into effect until after the close of this convention."

2. An incidental motion can be adopted that, in the event of the amendment's adoption, it shall not take effect until a specified time (597).

Either method requires only a majority vote.

What is the difference between a constitution and bylaws?

Nothing (12–15). In the old days, it was common practice to have both a constitution and bylaws. The organization's most essential rules were placed in the constitution to make them more difficult to amend (582). The distinction often confuses rather than clarifies, and the more current standard practice is that an organization's basic rules be placed in a single document called the *bylaws*.

The Chair

Any advice for the new chair?

For openers, the chair must be willing to do the job—must be willing to *lead*. There is a misconception that the chair is a closet fascist, a tyrant who uses the power of the office to abuse the rights of the grassroots members. Occasionally that is true. Far more likely is the chair who hesitates to lead, the chair who wants to please everyone and thus finds a way not to do the job. Our experience with presidents of organizations has been that almost universally they are concerned—at times obsessed—with being fair, with conducting business according to the rules. When the chair abuses the role or makes an error, motions are available in parliamentary procedure to correct the error; when the chair refuses to lead, the meeting dies (454–56).

How should the chair respond to the phrase "I so move" or "so moved"?

After an idea is stated (and sometimes before refinement), a member will push forward with the phrase, "I so move" or "So moved." Such a statement is as dangerous as the chair saying, "You have heard the motion." Neither approach provides the clarity necessary to avoid later confusion. "The chair should never try to avoid [this] critically important duty by saying, 'You have heard the motion' or by saying, 'The motion is moved and seconded' without repeating its words" (455).

May the chair enter into debate?

No, the presiding officer who wishes to debate must relinquish the chair and not return to it until the main question has been disposed of (43–44, 394–95). *Robert's* is strict: "On certain occasions—which should be extremely rare—the presiding officer may believe that a crucial factor relating to such a question has been overlooked and that his obligation as a member to call attention to the point outweighs his duty to preside at that time" (394–95). Too strict. The chair is not only a member; the chair is the *leader*. The chair has a responsibility to keep members fully informed of the consequences of any action they might take and may remain in the chair while meeting this responsibility. It does not serve the organization well to require the presiding officer to leave the chair while providing crucial information that is necessary for informed debate. For example, if a motion might prompt legal action due to proposed changes in state law, the presiding officer can and should call this situation to the attention of the members, and the members then can debate and act as they wish.

Should the chair say "Nay" or "No" for negative votes?

"No" is used in voice votes (45). The term "Nay" only appears occasionally in roll-call votes (420). Horses say "neigh"; people say "no." Oh, and while we are at it, the term "Aye" is pronounced like *eye*, not *hay*.

How should the chair phrase a rising or show of hands vote?

Once again, clarity is the key word. The chair should tell members *exactly* what she wishes them to do. For example, "The question is on the adoption of the motion to amend by ——." Those in favor of the motion to amend, please rise. . . . You may be seated. . . . Those opposed, please rise. . . . You may be seated." While this wording is slightly different from that found in *Robert's* (47), it has the advantage of sounding nicer. On a counted vote, the chair might add, "and remain standing while the vote is counted." Similarly for a vote by show of hands, "Those in favor of the motion, raise your hand. . . . Thank you. . . . Those opposed, raise your hand. . . . Thank you." Once again, *Robert's* has more detail (47), including which hand to raise, which is a bit unnecessary. Whichever voting method is used, always consider that some delegates due to infirmity or handicap may need a different means of expressing their vote.

May the chair of a small board (such as a condominium) make motions, enter into debate, and vote on motions?

Yes (487–88; also 9–10, 43, 53), subject to any specific rules or statutes to the contrary.

May the chair order the removal of a disruptive member?

No. Only the members have the right to require a member to leave a meeting. *Robert's* tests the patience of the chair with a multistep process:

- For a minor offense, a rap of the gavel and admonition to the member to avoid the fault may be sufficient;
- For a more serious offense, the chair can warn the member or call them to order ("The member is out of order and will be seated") and put to a vote whether the member may continue ("Shall the member be allowed to continue speaking?");
- For an especially grave offense, charges can be preferred and a penalty imposed by the body (645–48).

These steps may appear cumbersome in the face of a rowdy member, but *Robert's* process provides protection against a tyrannical chair. (See following question regarding alternatives to removal.)

May the chair order the removal of a disruptive nonmember?

A nonmember is a guest and if disruptive may be removed by order of the chair (644). Even in such an instance that seems to require removing a person from a meeting, the best advice is "Don't do it!" The possibility of violence or a lawsuit is just too great. Every step should be taken to diffuse the situation. Options might include taking a recess, taking a recess and speaking with the individual, taking a recess and having others speak with the individual, continuing the meeting to an adjourned meeting, or simply adjourning (if another regular meeting is scheduled). If anyone must be removed from a meeting, it is always best to use law enforcement or official security for the location.

What if the chair ignores a valid motion?

The first recourse is through a Point of Order. Depending on the chair's response to the Point of Order, an Appeal may be appropriate. *Robert's* also notes an instance when a member can process her own motion, though seldom used. "If the chair ignores a point of order that is not dilatory, the member can repeat the point of order a second and third time and if the chair still ignores it, the member, standing in his place, can immediately put the point of order to a vote without debate" (650).

The 11th Edition goes even further, adding a new section entitled "Removal of Presiding Officer from Chair for All or Part of a Session." This new language applies where the chair fails to act in compliance with an Appeal, a Point of Order submitted to the body, or "otherwise culpably fails to perform the duties of the chair properly in a meeting" (651). In instances of a temporary presiding officer, a motion to "declare the chair vacant and proceed to elect a new chairman" can be adopted by a majority vote (651). A permanent chair can have his authority to preside at part or all of a session removed by a motion to Suspend the Rules (652). Envisioning that these motions might not go over well, *Robert's* provides that once the motion is made the presiding officer must relinquish the chair, "and the remedy for refusal or failure to do so is that the motion may be put to a vote by its maker" (652).

What method can the chair use to facilitate recognizing members?

In a small body, recognition of members seeking to speak is not difficult. After all, there may only be one or two members attempting to claim the floor. However, if numerous members are seeking recognition, it can be difficult for the chair know who to call on next. Members who have not yet spoken have preference over those who have, and the chair is supposed to alternate the floor between those favoring and those opposing the measure (31). The chair can facilitate this process by asking at times, "Is there anyone who would like to speak who has not yet spoken?" or "Is there someone who would like to speak for [or "against"] the motion?"

Even these methods don't work well in large conventions where there are numerous microphones. Of even greater concern is that some motions are waived if not raised immediately (Point of Order, Division, Objection to Consideration). Without some process for recognizing such delegates immediately, an entire convention can become derailed. *Robert's* recognizes that in "large conventions or similar bodies, some of the rules applicable to the assignment of the floor may require adaptation" (383). Most often, this is accomplished by a card- or telephone-recognition system.

While there are several card-recognition systems, a common method is to have several card-stock colored cards attached to each microphone, such as green, red, yellow, and white. To speak in favor of a motion, a delegate raises a green card and awaits recognition. To speak against a motion, a delegate raises a red card and awaits recognition. The chair utilizes the green and red cards to alternate between pro and con speakers. Subsidiary motions, such as to Postpone Indefinitely, Refer, or Postpone, can be made on either a green or red card. The yellow card allows a member to "jump ahead" of delegates with green or red cards for certain motions, such as to ask a Request for Information or to Suspend the Rules. The white cards immediately interrupt all business and are used for urgent matters, such as a Point of Order, Appeal, or Objection to Consideration. On-stage spotters sometimes help the chair and parliamentarian keep track of speakers by arranging colored notecards in the correct order and handing them to the parliamentarian for review. Particularly for large conventions, the card-recognition system is an inexpensive means of alternating debate and recognizing certain motions more quickly.

Similar but more technologically sophisticated recognition methods include telephonic and computer-based processes. With either, delegates call-in or log-in a desire to speak along with the wording of any planned motions. These are organized in terms of when the slip arrives as well as the precedence of the motions and given to the parliamentarian for review.

Any closing tips for the chair?

Robert's has a good section on "Suggestions for Inexperienced Presiding Officers" on pages 454–56, which is a must read. The role of the chair as summed up in *Cannon's Concise Guide to Rules of Order* is "to provide a fair, democratic forum for debate of the issues at a meeting and to ensure an accurate count of the votes of the members. It's that simple! Once the members realize the Chair intends to fill that role, they support the Chair, allowing the person to move easily and freely in handling the business of the meeting."[97]

The Parliamentarian

What is the role of the parliamentarian?

Two misconceptions are held concerning the role of the parliamentarian. A common error occurs when the assembly argues about a point and then asks the parliamentarian for a ruling.

It is a great scene. The meeting is in a state of collapse, the delegates are exhausted from screaming and throwing things at one another, when a surviving delegate cries, "We want the parliamentarian's ruling." Sitting on a white horse offstage, the parliamentarian comes galloping onstage and pronounces a ruling, the delegates genuflect, and the hero rides off into the sunset. A decision has been made; order has been restored. As parliamentarians, we like that role. It provides us with attention, a sense of power, and the opportunity to display how much we know.

It is, unfortunately, an improper role for the parliamentarian.

The proper role of the parliamentarian is to *advise*; the parliamentarian *cannot rule* (466–67). Only the chair may rule on matters of procedure. Except in complex situations, the organization should not hear the voice of the parliamentarian.

A second misconception is that the parliamentarian serves only the chair. Closely related to this misconception is the image of the parliamentarian as one whose job is serving as a hired gun to wipe out any opposition to the president. The proper role of the parliamentarian is to *prevent* rather than to solve problems, and this is accomplished by serving not only the chair but also every member of the organization (466–67).[98] *Robert's* supports this position by noting that a parliamentarian can advise "the president and other officers, committees, and members on matters of parliamentary procedure" (465).

The parliamentarian cannot run around among the assembly, leaving the chair at the mercy of an unexpected Point of Order. But by using discretion, the parliamentarian can serve delegates who ask questions during breaks or come to the front. Delegates must understand that the parliamentarian might have to leave abruptly to aid the chair.

An assembly of delegates is a curious body. The chair wants to create a chemistry of movement, of progress, of getting things done. Each time the chair stops to consult the parliamentarian, she risks breaking and thus losing that mood. Once the mood is broken, it is difficult to reclaim. Therefore, the good parliamentarian does more than wait to be asked for an opinion but is always at least one step ahead of the meeting, ready to signal the chair of an impending problem. Like the ghostwriter to the public speaker, the parliamentarian's role is to function in such a way that all attention and credit is directed to the chair. In effect, the role of the parliamentarian is to make the presiding officer look good.

The parliamentarian advises and serves the chair; and the best way to advise and serve the chair is to advise and serve every member, so that questions and problems are answered and solved without interrupting the business of the assembly.

What if the parliamentarian's advice is ignored by the chair?

Those are the breaks. "After the parliamentarian has expressed an opinion on a point, the chair has the duty to make the final ruling and, in doing so, has the right to follow the advice of the parliamentarian or to disregard it" (467).

What should a parliamentarian review prior to a convention?

The parliamentarian should study

the constitution and/or bylaws of the society;

any special and/or standing rules (including convention standing rules);

other governing documents as appropriate, such as corporate charters or articles of incorporation;

the transcript (or if not available, minutes) of the preceding convention;

the adopted parliamentary authority;

any items noticed for the convention, such as bylaws amendments, resolutions, legislative proposals, or new business items; and

minutes of board meetings prior to the convention.

Who should the parliamentarian meet with prior to a convention?

At a minimum, the parliamentarian should meet with the president, and depending on the circumstances and the anticipated business/problems, with the vice president, the board, committee chairs, executive director, and/or legal counsel, before the convention.

The intent of these meetings is to review the procedures and customs of the organization; to see that all officers have done their jobs; and to ensure that the president is prepared for any question concerning the impact of one business item on another (608–9). For example, does the adoption or rejection of any proposed bylaw amendment affect any other proposed bylaw amendment? What is the budgetary impact of any resolution or new business item, or what will be the procedure for implementing any motion that is adopted? When the chair must repeatedly stop the business of the convention to find the answers to such questions, it is a sign that the leadership has not done its homework.

While a president may first decline to meet because of a busy schedule leading up to a convention, usually a parliamentarian can gently point out the value of such a meeting, especially in anticipating and managing difficult and challenging issues, and the president will subsequently agree to meet.

How may a parliamentarian keep track of the parliamentary situation?

In large assemblies and conventions, it can be important for the parliamentarian to keep track of both motions made and who has spoken. Such information can assist the chair in assigning the floor (since debate should alternate and no one should speak twice to the same motion), and it can be lifesaving in the event of later motions to Reconsider (both for determining who spoke earlier as well whether the motion to Reconsider is timely in a multiday convention). Although formats vary, many parliamentarians keep a "Parliamentarian's Log," which summarizes each motion made, whether it was seconded, who debated on each side of the motion, as well as any secondary motions, and whether the motion was adopted or rejected.[99]

How should the chair and parliamentarian communicate during a meeting?

According to *Robert's*, it is "also the duty of the parliamentarian—as inconspicuously as possible—to call the attention of the chair to any error in the proceedings that may affect the substantive rights of any member or may otherwise do harm" (466). However, "in advising the chair, the parliamentarian should not wait until asked for advice— that may be too late" (466). As a result, some professional parliamentarians utilize methods for communicating—as inconspicuously as possible—throughout the business portion of a convention. Parliamentarians have several techniques for doing this.

Some parliamentarians use a type of card system (as described in *Cannon's Concise Guide to Rules of Order*).[100] Such cards are often note-sized and have a brief, or shorthand, description of the wording to process any motion. While the cards can be handed to the presiding officer, they are often clipped or attached to the lectern so that all cards are visible to the presiding officer at all times. The chair, by glancing at the lectern, can see the order of all pending motions as well as the specific wording for each.

For instance, the card for handling an Appeal might read as follows:

APPEAL (§ 24)

Is there a second?
There is an appeal from the decision of the chair.

The question is, "Shall the decision of the chair be sustained?"

Is there any debate? (if debatable)

(When debate is finished)

The question is, "Shall the decision of the chair be sustained?"

Those in favor of sustaining the decision of the chair, say *aye*.

Those *opposed* to sustaining the decision of the chair, say *no*.

The decision of the chair is [not] sustained.

Majority Vote

Similarly, a card for taking the vote on the motion to Amend might read:

AMEND (§ 12)

**The question is on the adoption of the motion to amend by
_____.**

Those in favor of the motion to amend, say *aye*.

Those opposed, say *no*.

The amendment is [not] adopted.

Debatable
Majority Vote

Our experience is that the card system is professional, flexible, and inconspicuous. While the presiding officer is conducting the meeting, it is with the assistance of the parliamentarian. The chair should be familiar with the cards before the convention begins. Otherwise, the cards will appear as a foreign object rather than an aid. The key for the chair: trust the cards.

Other parliamentarians—especially for unusual or complex motions—prefer fuller scripts. As noted by Nancy Sylvester in *The Guerilla Guide to Robert's Rules*, a script gives the chair "not only the correct words to say but the confidence to say them."[101] Motions, reports of committees, and even entire conventions can be scripted.

Where should the parliamentarian sit?

While it may seem obvious, the parliamentarian "should be seated next to the presiding officer" (609). An older practice in some conventions was for the parliamentarian to be on stage, but not close to the presiding officer. Of course, such an arrangement is of little help to the presiding officer in the event of a procedural dispute. Also, if someone must "get" the parliamentarian, it draws too much attention to the fact that the chair needs parliamentary assistance.

What other services may a parliamentarian provide in addition to assisting at meetings?

There is no set rule on the number of functions a parliamentarian may be asked to perform, but responsibilities can include

Assisting committee chairs with wording for reports and motions
Advising on bylaws and bylaws amendments
Working on constitution and bylaws revisions
Conferring with the chair during breaks in order to anticipate
    upcoming issues or potential problems
Advising on the language of presiding scripts
Assisting or supervising with elections as to procedural aspects
    (blank vs. illegal vs. ineligible ballots, language used during
    election, etc.)
Advising on parliamentary tactics and strategy
Conducting training/workshops for officers, board members, or
    leaders on running effective meetings
Providing formal parliamentary opinions
Serving as an expert witness regarding procedure

May a parliamentarian advise on laws and statutes?

Some attorneys are parliamentarians, but not all parliamentarians
are attorneys. Unfortunately, at times the distinction between a parliamentary opinion and a legal opinion can be fine. Federal labor
laws impact unions, and state statutes impact homeowner and condominium associations, nonprofit corporations, and governmental
bodies. As a result, while parliamentarians should be cautious when
giving parliamentary advice to these types of entities, they should at
least be aware of statutes affecting the procedural functioning of the
organization. If a parliamentary question involves a statute or law
and there is no time to consult the organization's attorney, the parliamentarian should provide as thorough an answer as possible using
governing documents, parliamentary authorities, and knowledge.
Then, the parliamentarian should inform the client of the existence
of the statute or law and that legal issues are involved on which an
attorney should be consulted.

May a parliamentarian preside at a meeting?

At times, the contentiousness, complexity, or politics of a situation
may call for an outside chair. In such instances, a parliamentarian may
be asked to serve as a professional presiding officer. The 11th Edition
includes a new heading, "Invited Temporary Presiding Officer" (453).
According to *Robert's*, such an arrangement can be accomplished by

majority vote if the "president and the vice-president(s) do not object" or by a motion to Suspend the Rules, "even over the objection of the president or a vice-president" (453–54).

What are the obligations of the parliamentarian if a member of the assembly?

Without question, a member parliamentarian has the potential for a conflict (or at least the appearance of conflict) of interest when issues come before the body. *Robert's* attempts to address this by imposing on the member parliamentarian similar responsibility for impartiality as that of the chair. A member parliamentarian "does not make motions, participate in debate, or vote on any question except in the case of a ballot vote" (467).

What books should every parliamentarian own?

Other than this one? A parliamentarian should have access to the following materials:

Henry M. Robert III, Daniel H. Honemann, and Thomas J. Balch, *Robert's Rules of Order Newly Revised* (11th ed.). Don't leave home without it.

Henry M. Robert III, William J. Evans, Daniel H. Honemann, and Thomas J. Balch, *Robert's Rules of Order Newly Revised: In Brief* (2nd ed.). A shorter introduction to *Robert's*.

Alice Sturgis, *The Standard Code of Parliamentary Procedure* (4th ed., revised by the AIP). Sturgis's first edition was a major contribution to those seeking a more readable text on parliamentary law and practice. Revised by the American Institute of Parliamentarians, the fourth edition published in 2001 provides a well-written alternative or companion to *Robert's*. Of special interest to those who adopt *Robert's* as their authority is Chapter 29, "Functioning under *Robert's Rules of Order*." Also of particular value is Chapter 30, "Often-Asked Questions."

American Institute of Parliamentarians, *American Institute of Parliamentarians Standard Code of Parliamentary Procedure*. The *AIPSC* is a new work (published in 2012) based on the principles of simplification, modernization, and ease of comprehension enunciated by Alice Sturgis.

George Demeter, *Demeter's Manual of Parliamentary Law and
Procedure*. While out-of-print, *Demeter's Manual* is an excellent
source to use when double-checking an answer to complicated
problems.

Jim Slaughter, *The Complete Idiot's Guide to Parliamentary Procedure Fast-Track*. The first book in a new *Fast-Track* series (published 2012) designed to get you up and running for your next
meeting as quickly as possible.

Additional sources include three books of parliamentary opinions
from national parliamentary organizations:

National Association of Parliamentarians, *Parliamentary Questions
and Answers,* volume 4.

Virginia Schlotzhauer, William J. Evans, and John R. Stipp, *Parliamentary Opinions: A Compilation and Revision of the Opinions
Committee, 1958 to 1982.*

Virginia Schlotzhauer, Margaret A. Banks, Floyd M. Riddick, and
John R. Stipp, *Parliamentary Opinions II: Solutions to Problems
of Organizations.*

These books can supplement the procedures found in *Robert's*.
Also, by seeing where and how they differ, you will have a better understanding of *why* things are done the way they are done. As stated
by one parliamentarian, "Unless the reason for a rule is understood,
it is difficult to learn the rule, and it is still more difficult to apply it
successfully in practice."[102] Finally, as stated earlier in this book, it
never hurts to know more than you need to know.

What else should a parliamentarian study?

Two national organizations certify parliamentarians as well as provide programming and publications in parliamentary procedure: the
National Association of Parliamentarians and the American Institute
of Parliamentarians.

National Association of Parliamentarians (NAP)

The National Association of Parliamentarians was founded in Octo-
ber 1930 in Kansas City, Missouri, and is the oldest and largest nonprofit parliamentary organization. NAP publishes a quarterly journal,
National Parliamentarian, which consists of educational articles on

parliamentary procedure as well as administrative articles on the activities of NAP and its chapters.

Classifications of NAP membership include Regular, Honorary, and Credentialed. Credentialed membership levels include Registered Parliamentarian (RP), Professional Registered Parliamentarian (PRP), and Retired Credentialed Parliamentarian. There is an examination requirement for NAP membership based upon the latest edition of *Robert's*.

National Association of Parliamentarians
213 South Main Street,
Independence, MO 64050–3850
888-NAP-2929
www.parliamentarians.org

American Institute of Parliamentarians (AIP)

The American Institute of Parliamentarians was founded in Chicago in 1958. Robert W. English is credited with founding AIP. Traditionally, a distinction between the organizations has been a greater emphasis in AIP on parliamentary authorities beyond *Robert's*.

AIP may be best known for its parliamentary practicums. Practicums are multiday programs offering intensive education in parliamentary procedure, including lectures, workshops, and group projects.

AIP publishes a quarterly journal, *Parliamentary Journal*, which consists of educational articles on parliamentary procedure. A newsletter entitled *The Communicator* is published quarterly with administrative articles on the activities of AIP and its chapters.

Classifications of AIP membership at the individual level include Regular, Certified Parliamentarian (CP), Certified Professional Parliamentarian (CPP), Retired, and Full-time Student. There is also an Associate membership for associations, institutions, or corporations. CPs and CPPs may complete an additional program for designation as a "Teacher" of parliamentary procedure. There is no examination requirement for AIP membership.

American Institute of Parliamentarians
550M Ritchie Hwy, #271
Severna Park, MD 21146
888–664–0428
www.aipparl.org

Parliamentary Web Sites

www.aipparl.org—American Institute of Parliamentarians.

www.e-aip.org—Electronic Chapter of the American Institute of Parliamentarians.

www.jimslaughter.com—Web site of Jim Slaughter, which includes many charts and articles on meeting procedures, references, and links to parliamentary resources.

www.notesonrobertsrules.com—Web site of *Notes and Comments on Robert's Rules* (4th edition).

www.parliamentarians.org—National Association of Parliamentarians.

www.parliamentarylawyers.org—American College of Parliamentary Lawyers.

www.robertsrules.com—Official Robert's Rules of Order Web site.

http://groups.yahoo.com/group/parliamentary—Online discussion of parliamentary law and procedure, including various parliamentary authorities.

http://sites.google.com/site/enapunit—Electronic Unit of the National Association of Parliamentarians (eNAP).

NOTES

REFERENCES

INDEX

Notes

Introduction

1. Henry Martyn Robert abbreviated the title of his original work *R.O.* for *Rules of Order*. His 1915 revision, *Robert's Rules of Order Revised*, then became abbreviated *R.O.R.* Editions since 1970 titled *Robert's Rules of Order Newly Revised* are usually abbreviated *RONR* (without periods). The 11th Edition recommends a citation of *RONR* (11th ed.) with page and line numbers. In this book, we use the term *Robert's* to refer to the 11th Edition (2011), and the name "Robert" for the original author, Henry Martyn Robert. Specific references to the 11th Edition are used to highlight a change from previous editions.

2. Parliamentary authors have long advocated simplified meeting procedures. Thomas Jefferson explained the purpose of his 1801 *Manual of Parliamentary Practice* in its preface: "I have begun a sketch, which those who come after me will successively correct and fill up, till a code of rules shall be formed . . . the effects of which may be, accuracy in business, economy of time, order, uniformity, and impartiality." Even Henry Martyn Robert wrote his *Rules of Order* because he saw the need for a modern, simple code of parliamentary procedure for voluntary organizations. Someday, someone or some association may write a new code of parliamentary procedure that will replace *Robert's*. Maybe. But today, people want more than simple procedure; they want an understandable *Robert's*.

3. Herman W. Farwell, *The Majority Rules: A Manual of Procedure for Most Groups* (Pueblo, Colo.: High Publishers, 1980), 1. For a few examples of parliamentary manuals that serve as introductory guides and attempt to simplify parliamentary procedure, see Jim Slaughter, *The Complete Idiot's Guide to Parliamentary Procedure Fast-Track* (New York: Penguin, 2012); Nancy Sylvester, *The Complete Idiot's Guide to Robert's Rules*, 2nd ed. (New York: Penguin, 2010); C. Allan Jennings, *Robert's Rules for Dummies* (Hoboken, N.J.: Wiley, 2005); James Lochrie, *Meeting Procedures: Parliamentary Law and Rules of Order for the 21st Century* (Lanham, Md.: Scarecrow, 2003). Alice Sturgis, with her two editions of *Sturgis Standard Code of Parliamentary Procedure* (New York: McGraw-Hill, 1950 and 1966), has received credit for modernizing terminology while at the same time retaining nearly all the traditional motions. The 3rd (1988) and 4th (2001) editions, revised under the auspices of the American Institute of Parliamentarians (AIP), retained her approach to modernize terminology and eliminated several motions and devices. A new work, the *American Institute of Parliamentarians Standard Code of Parliamentary Procedure* (2012), is based on the principles of simplification, modernization, and

ease of comprehension enunciated by Alice Sturgis. If Henry A. Davidson had written his book, *Handbook of Parliamentary Procedure* (New York: Ronald Press, 1968), with the flair that he displayed in his articles, he might have received more notice and credit for modernizing procedure; see, for example, "Let's Modernize Parliamentary Terminology," *Parliamentary Journal* 2 (Jan. 1962), 3–10; "General Robert Rode a Buggy," *Parliamentary Journal* 7 (Jan. 1966), 8–12; and "Towards a More Informal Procedure," *Parliamentary Journal* 12 (Jan. 1971), 10, 31. Gregg Phifer was a tireless voice for reform; see, for example, "Trends in Parliamentary Procedure: Future Form and Practice," *Parliamentary Journal* 28 (Apr. 1987), 59–66. Much credit, commentary, and criticism for writing a modern introductory and simple code goes to Ray E. Keesey, *Modern Parliamentary Procedure* (Boston: Houghton Mifflin, 1974). While many parliamentarians talked about the need for a modern code, Keesey wrote one. Credit for generating enthusiasm for and specific ideas about a modern code should go to Robert W. English, the sometimes crusty founder of the American Institute of Parliamentarians. In the final analysis, no one person can be singled out as the originator of "modern" parliamentary procedure.

4. Repeated surveys of parliamentarians have shown *Robert's* as the manual of choice. In a 1970 study by the American Institute of Parliamentarians, 85 to 90.5 percent of certified professional parliamentarians responding listed *Robert's* as the manual of authority. See Emogene Emery, "AIP's Response to *RONR*," *Parliamentary Journal* 12 (Apr. 1971), 8–11. Another survey thirty years later revealed *Robert's* still around 90 percent. See Jim Slaughter, "Parliamentary Practices of CPP's in 2000," *Parliamentary Journal*, 42 (Jan. 2001), 1–11. With several long-time competitors to *Robert's* having gone out of print, it is likely its percentage is the same or higher.

5. Four books come to mind: Farwell's *Majority Rules*, "designed for most groups or clubs of today with memberships of somewhere between ten and twenty-five individuals" (3); Davidson's *Handbook of Parliamentary Procedure*, which "aims to present in simple step-by-step terms the rules and practices of parliamentary procedure for the small organization—the local business association, professional or scientific society, union, civic group, lodge, and social club" (v); Doris P. Zimmerman's *Robert's Rules in Plain English*, 2nd ed. (New York: HarperCollins, 2005), "for the small informal society" (xvi); and Arthur T. Lewis and Henry M. Robert's, *Robert's Rules Simplified* (Mineola, N.Y.: Dover Publications, 2006), 1–4.

6. Marshall Soren, "Robert's Rules of Order Newly Revised: A Review," *Parliamentary Journal* 11 (Apr. 1970), 17.

7. Soren, "A Review," 19, 20.

8. See Emogene Emery, "AIP's Response to *RONR*," *Parliamentary Journal* 12 (Apr. 1971), 8–11 (citing that 85 percent of the leadership of the American Institute of Parliamentarians was disappointed that the terminology in the 1970 revision had not been modernized).

9. Arguing about *Robert's Rules* has been a long-standing debate among parliamentarians. For example, Edwin C. Bliss notes, "the issue of Robert vs. Sturgis hasn't had quite as much publicity as Roe vs. Wade, but in some circles it's

almost as controversial." "'User-Friendly' Parliamentary Procedure: A Rebuttal," *Parliamentary Journal* 33 (Apr. 1992), 78–80. See also Gregg Phifer, "The Robert Heirs Blew It," *Parliamentary Journal* 23 (July 1982), 81–91, for a robust discussion of *Robert's* strengths and weaknesses. Or, ten years later, Nancy Sylvester, "Robert Is the Only Choice," *Parliamentary Journal* 33 (Jan. 1992), 3–9; and Gregg Phifer, "Maybe Robert Is Not the Worst Choice, But . . . ," *Parliamentary Journal* 33 (Apr. 1992), 66–74. With the tenth edition of *Robert's* (2000) and the fourth edition of the AIP's *The Standard Code of Parliamentary Procedure* (2001), students of parliamentary procedure received more of the same. And with 120 noted changes in the new *Robert's*, including renaming Point of Information to Request for Information, continuing debate remains ensured.

10. James W. Cleary, "A Commentary on Robert's Rules of Order Newly Revised," *Parliamentary Journal* 9 (Apr. 1968), 8, 9.

11. William J. Evans, "Concerning *ROR Newly Revised*," *Parliamentary Journal* 10 (Oct. 1969), 8, 12.

12. Henry M. Robert III, William J. Evans, and Ray E. Keesey, "The Rules: Can They Cope?" *Parliamentary Journal* 12 (Jan. 1971), 10.

13. Henry M. Robert III, "Revising RONR: What We Can and Cannot Do," *National Parliamentarian,* First Quarter 2007, 6–15. The coauthor articulates five reasons for making changes in subsequent editions: (1) applying existing principles to newly arising questions; (2) recognizing new practices that have reached established status; (3) correcting inconsistencies or ambiguities; (4) altering arrangement or presentation; or (5) giving clearer or expanded explanations. These five reasons have been articulated again for the 11th Edition in Henry M. Robert III, "Guiding Principles for Changes in New Editions of Robert's Rules of Order Newly Revised," *National Parliamentarian*, First Quarter 2012, 7–13.

Part I

14. Except where noted otherwise, all parenthetical page references are to *Robert's Rules of Order Newly Revised*, 11th edition (2011).

15. To ensure understanding of this all-important concept, those interested may wish to review James Lochrie, *Meeting Procedures: Parliamentary Law and Rules of Order for the 21st Century* (Lanham, Md.: Scarecrow, 2003), 48–51, and Shmuel Gerber, "Rungs of the Ladder: Precedence of Subsidiary Motions," *Parliamentary Journal* 48 (July 2007), 98–107. See also Richard S. Kain, "Analogy in the Teaching of Precedence," *Parliamentary Journal* 6 (Apr. 1965), 23–27. For a criticism of the concept, see Hugo E. Hellman, "Robert's Precedence Is Nonsense," *Parliamentary Journal* 12 (Apr. 1971), 3–7.

Robert's lists seven subsidiary motions (63–64). The number of possible motions increases when the amending process and the qualified call for the previous question are included. When primary and secondary amendments to amendable subsidiary motions are added, there are fourteen subsidiary motions (65). See J. Calvin Callaghan, "Precedence in Parliamentary Motions,"

Parliamentary Journal 7 (Apr. 1966), 21–26; or Haig Bosmajian, *Readings in Parliamentary Procedure* (New York: Harper and Row, 1968), 175–80. When the qualified call for the previous question is added, there are twenty-six subsidiary motions. See George Demeter, "Twenty-Six Subsidiary Motions Pending at Once," *Parliamentary Journal* 12 (July 1971), 16 (reprinted in *Parliamentary Journal* 52 (Apr. 2011), 80). When the qualified motion to Limit or Extend Limits of Debate and primary and secondary amendments to amendable privileged motions are added, the chart of parliamentary motions becomes a scroll.

Part II

16. The following motions, requests, or calls do not require a second:
    Call a member to order
    Call for a separate vote on a resolution that is one of a series on different subjects offered by a single motion
    Call for the Orders of the Day
    Call up a motion to Reconsider
    Call up a motion to Reconsider and Enter on the Minutes
    Division of the Assembly
    Nomination
    Objection to the Consideration of a Question
    Parliamentary Inquiry
    Point of Order
    Proposal for Filling a Blank
    Question of Privilege
    Request for Information
    Request for Permission to Withdraw or Modify a Motion
    Request to Be Excused from a Duty
    Request to Read Papers

17. Robert English, founder of the American Institute of Parliamentarians, provides four reasons for abolishing seconds:

1. It *eliminates an unnecessary complication.* The old rule requiring a second did not apply to committees and did not apply to many secondary motions even in assemblies, e.g.; "Division of the Assembly"; "Consider Seriatim"; "Call up a Motion to Reconsider"; "Make a Nomination"; "Request for Information"; "Point of Order"; "Request Permission to Withdraw Motion." Motions to approve recommendations of a committee also did not require a second. There were so many exceptions that few experts could keep them straight!

2. It *saves time.* Under the old rules, there were frequent delays to secure a second and in many cases a delay to secure the name of the seconder. Meetings were even interrupted after a vote on a motion by a Point of Order claiming that the motion was never seconded!

3. It *removes an unwise deterrent to the making of motions.* In a majority of meetings, there is too much timidity about making motions from the floor. For example, a member may realize that a pending main motion needs to be amended, but does not move to Amend for fear that his motion will not be seconded.

4. It *lessens the temptation of debating a motion before making it.* Under the old rules, members often discuss their motions before making them in order to ensure a second.

The chief alleged advantage of requiring a second is to avoid requiring the body to consider undesirable motions. Actual experience indicates that this old rule rarely served as an effective deterrent of undesirable motions. Of course there is need for reasonable protection against the waste of time with motions clearly not worth consideration. But such waste of time has been rarely prevented by the rule requiring a second. The chief waste of time is due to discussion with no motion pending and with no definite issue up for discussion.

In mature organizations, most main motions arise out of committee reports, which require no additional second from the floor. Debatable secondary motions (e.g., Amend, Refer, Postpone) are usually relevant to the pending main motion and therefore may be discussed by a member before he makes the secondary motion. If a member wishes to present a very unpopular motion, he usually can get a friend to second it. Rarely does the requirement of a second prevent the assembly from considering an undesirable motion. More often it prevents desirable motions from being made. (English, Modern Code, 14–15.)

Thais M. Plaisted ("The When, the Why, and the Where of the Second," *Parliamentary Journal* 19 [Oct. 1978], 16–17) and Keesey (*Modern Parliamentary Procedure,* 31–32) also argue that the second should be abolished.

18. Jon Ericson, "Misunderstanding Democracy: How Many Delegates Does It Take to Move a Motion?," *Parliamentary Journal* 44 (Apr. 2003), 57–63.

19. Dominic Holzhaus, "Whose Motion Is It Anyway?," *Parliamentary Journal* 50 (July 2012), 83–90. Barry Glazer, "Negative Motion, No Motion, What Can We Do?," *Parliamentary Journal* 52 (Apr. 2011), 76–79.

20. American Institute of Parliamentarians, *The Standard Code of Parliamentary Procedure* (4th ed.), 244, hereafter cited as *The Standard Code,* 4th edition. A closely related text published in 2012, the *American Institute of Parliamentarians Standard Code of Parliamentary Procedure,* will be cited as *Standard Code AIP.* For some differences in the new work, see Jim Lochrie, "American Institute of Parliamentarians Standard Code of Parliamentary Procedure," *Parliamentary Journal* 53 (Jan. 2012), 29–33.

21. Higher procedural authorities can supersede provisions in *Robert's.* Federal labor laws govern unions; and state statutes impact city councils, school boards,

county commissions, legislative bodies, community (homeowner and condominium) associations, and nonprofit corporations. See Model Nonprofit Corporation Act Subcommittee, Committee on Nonprofit Organizations, ABA Section of Business Law, "Changes in the Model Nonprofit Corporation Act—Miscellaneous and Technical Amendments," *Business Lawyer* 67, Feb. 2012, 473-89; Michael E. Malamut, "District of Columbia Enacts Member-Friendly Nonprofit Corporation Law, Part I," *National Parliamentarian*, Second Quarter 2011, 11–15; Michael E. Malamut, "District of Columbia Enacts Member-Friendly Nonprofit Corporation Law, Part II," *National Parliamentarian*, Third Quarter 2011, 30–35; Michael E. Malamut, "District of Columbia Enacts Member-Friendly Nonprofit Corporation Law, Part III," *National Parliamentarian*, Fourth Quarter 2011, 8–12; Michael E. Malamut, "Issues of Concern to Parliamentarians Raised by the 2008 Revision of the Model Nonprofit Corporation Act," *National Parliamentarian*, First Quarter 2009, 24–31; Michael E. Malamut, "Issues of Concern to Parliamentarians Raised by the 1952 Model Nonprofit Corporation Act," *National Parliamentarian*, Third Quarter 2008, 16–21; James H. Slaughter, "Statutes and Procedures of Community Associations," *National Parliamentarian*, First Quarter 2005, 9–14; James H. Slaughter, "Avoid the Practice of Law," *National Parliamentarian*, First Quarter 2003, 16–18; James H. Slaughter, "Community Associations and the Parliamentarian," *National Parliamentarian*, First Quarter 2000, 25–28. Unless otherwise noted, answers in *Notes and Comments* are based solely on *Robert's* and do not address statutes or other governing documents such as bylaws, convention rules, or adopted special rules of order.

22. Kim Goldsworthy, "'All Opposed, Same Sign'—What?," *Parliamentary Journal* 51 (Oct. 2010), 141–44.

23. Paul McClintock, "History of 'Aye' and 'No,'" *Parliamentary Journal* 51 (Jan. 2010), 35–37.

Part III

24. *The Standard Code,* 4th edition, 34; *Standard Code AIP,* 37.

25. See George Demeter, "Resolutions Can Circumvent Main Motion," *Parliamentary Journal* 13 (Jan. 1972), 25.

26. "After listening to concerns about the proposed policy's adverse effects, [one board member] said, 'who can vote against good nutrition? It's almost like voting against God, motherhood and apple pie with honey on it.'" Rather than Postpone Indefinitely, however, the board chose to refer the matter to committee. Melinda Voss, "School Board Refuses to Enact Junk Food Ban," *Des Moines Tribune,* 2 July 1980.

27. The motion to Postpone Indefinitely was under attack at least as early as 1909:

> Parliamentary law is still developing on what may be called its moral side, and a pertinent illustration is in the disuse of the motion to postpone indefinitely. The objections are that the motion is both needless and immoral. On its face, it purports to be a courteous and

not unfriendly motion to delay till later, as if it might permit the subject to be taken up again. But that purpose is amply met by the motion to lay on the table. The motion to postpone indefinitely has that character of friendly hatred which requires solicitously, "Art thou in health, my brother?" and drives the knife up to the hilt under the fifth rib. Again, it gives its supporters two opportunities to vote upon their real proposition. If they are defeated at first on the motion to postpone indefinitely, they can hustle for a majority on the straight yea and nay vote. If they win by means of their plausibly and deceitfully worded motion, the subject-matter is as dead as if it had been struck on the head by a broad axe. It is probably the fact that the smooth wording of the motion secures votes which a direct "no" would not secure, and yet the effect of the vote, when carried, is precisely the same as a straight "no." Therefore the motion has been discarded as not to be tolerated by honorable men. (Raymond L. Bridgman, "Parliamentary Law: A World Institution," *Bibliothecca Sacra* 66 [Oct. 1909], 659–60.)

Sixty-four years later, the motion was still under attack. Leaving aside the question of morality and lacking only Bridgman's metaphor, Darwin Patnode stated his opinion of the motion to Postpone Indefinitely: "The motion to postpone indefinitely is an insult to the intelligence embodied in most parliamentary rules; is without redeeming parliamentary value of any valid sort; and is misleading to the point of becoming a true burden," and he concludes "that the motion to postpone indefinitely is improperly titled, easily replaceable, and inconsistent with other rules that parliamentarians unhesitatingly endorse." ("Opinions," *Parliamentary Journal* 14 [Jan. 1973], 20, 21). The 3rd edition of the *Standard Code* eliminated Postpone Indefinitely but made matters worse by recommending that "when a motion is made to postpone indefinitely, the chair handle it as a motion to table" (225). In the 4th edition, the authors retained this position but did so indirectly: "Most organizations . . . simply table a motion they do not want to vote on directly. This is technically a violation of *Robert's Rules*, but the prohibition is simply ignored in most organizations" (235).

28. Davidson, "General Robert Rode a Buggy," 8–12, attacks *Robert's* for allowing an amendment to be hostile but not negative. His article is a delight to read, and the reader should hear his case:

> Now tighten your seat belt, because . . . we are told that "a resolution of censure may be amended by striking out the word 'censure' and inserting the word 'thanks.'" If that isn't converting an affirmative into a negative, I'd like to know what is. (I predict the answer for some of the disciples: the negative of "I move a vote of thanks," would be "I move a vote of no thanks," and this would be forbidden; but "I move a vote of censure" is acceptable.) It is both unconscionable and inefficient to allow a vote of commendation to be converted into a

vote of condemnation by a one-word amendment. It is inefficient, because the antagonistic members should express themselves simply by voting "no" on the commendation. That is simple, honorable and unconfusing. The sacred writings, however, allow them to vent their spleen by amending "commend" to "condemn"—a messy and inefficient operation. And it is unconscionable to give the opponents of the measure a free ride on a horse supplied by its friends.

Davidson's argument leads him to conclude, in *Handbook of Parliamentary Procedure*, "The rule then is this: the maker of a motion is entitled to have the meeting vote on that motion or on a substantially similar version of it. He cannot be compelled to forego this by an amendment which destroys or negates the obvious intent of his original motion" (116). Davidson, then, makes no distinction between specific and general intent. For an analysis of "*Robert's* obvious inferiority [in the area of germaneness]," see Darwin Patnode, "Criteria for Germaneness of Amendments," *Parliamentary Journal* 13 (Apr. 1972), 14–18. For another example, see Virginia Schlotzhauer, William J. Evans, and John R. Stipp, *Parliamentary Opinions: A Compilation and Revision of the Opinions Committee 1958 to 1982* (Fort Wayne, Ind.: American Institute of Parliamentarians, 1982), 79, question 152.

29. Lena LaNelle Hardcastle, *By the Rule: Parliamentary Law Motions Made Easy* (Garland, Tex: Stuart Books, 1974), 85.

30. For a criticism of *Robert's* amending process within the perfecting process, see Wayne E. Hoogestraat, "Secondary Amendments to a Main Motion?" *Parliamentary Journal* 21 (July 1980), 32–33. For the argument that the perfecting process should be abolished, see Robert W. English, "A New View of Subsidiary Motions," *Parliamentary Journal* 10 (Jan. 1969), 21–22: "If [the perfecting process] is logically and efficiently used, the result is likely to be that the main motion as amended and the substitute (as amended) are substantially or identically the same. Then, after ill-conceived delay and complications, we have the ridiculous situation of choosing between two motions which are the same!"

31. Later, *Robert's* adds that creating a blank might also be helpful with the motion to refer to committee (173–74). See Jeannette Collins, "Opinions," *Parliamentary Journal* 10 (Apr. 1969), 30–32, question 44.

32. For a different answer see Schlotzhauer, Evans, and Stipp, *Parliamentary Opinions*, 93, question 54.

33. Doris Abbate, "Greatest Flexibility—Creating and Filling a Blank," *Parliamentary Journal* 53 (Jan. 2012), 34–40. For a demonstration of creating and filling a blank, see William Dixon Southworth, "Creating and Filling Blanks," *Parliamentary Journal* 34 (Apr. 1993), 71–74. See also Byrl A. Whitney, "'Filling Blanks': An Efficient Technique," *Parliamentary Journal* 5 (Oct. 1964), 7:

> It has been charged that parliamentary law does not permit . . . sufficient flexibility of choice in group decision making. It is not parliamentary law that produces this result, but ignorance of it. . . . [O]rganization

leaders strive to build organizations with inadequate knowledge either of the existence or the manner of use of essential "tools" provided by parliamentary law. "Simplified" books on the subject, and even teachers of Parliamentary Law, fail to mention many of these valuable tools.... FILLING BLANK procedure is one of the most efficient tools in the whole kit of parliamentary tools wherever the selection of one of several alternatives is required. The ordinary amending process fails to meet the need in such a situation.

34. *The Standard Code*, for example, states, "A committee report cannot be amended except by the committee" (*The Standard Code*, 4th edition, 187; *Standard Code AIP*, 201). George Demeter (*Demeter's Manual*) says, "You cannot amend any committee report unless its facts are wrong" (279). *Robert's* provides greater latitude, beginning with counseling against the adoption of a committee report: "In rare instances . . . [the assembly] may have occasion to adopt the (entire) report," but "adoption of an entire report is seldom wise" (507–8). Then he states, "An assembly that is to adopt an entire report which it has received can amend the report, but the text as published or recorded must not make the reporting board or committee appear to say anything different from the wording that was actually reported" (509).

35. Henry M. Robert in *Parliamentary Law* notes that the minority on a committee "have not the right to make a minority report, but the privilege is rarely refused" (269).

36. Mary D. Smith, "A Comparison between the Committee of the Whole and Its Alternate Forms in RONR," *Parliamentary Journal* 46 (July 2005), 112–17.

37. The 3rd edition of *The Standard Code* comments on "the absurdity of this procedure" (222). The 4th edition drops any talk about "absurdity" and suggests that a motion to resolve into a committee of the whole be treated as a motion to consider informally (232–33). *Riddick's Rules of Procedure: A Modern Guide to Faster and More Efficient Meetinvgs* (New York: Charles Scribner's Sons, 1985) also discards committee of the whole and quasi committee of the whole and retains consider informally (56).

38. Keesey, *Modern Parliamentary Procedure*, 90; *The Standard Code*, 4th edition, 232; Lochrie, *Meeting Procedures*, 44.

39. Mason, "The Legal Side of Parliamentary Procedure," 52. For additional background on Henry Martyn Robert, see Donald Fishman, "The Elusive Henry Martyn Robert: A Historical Problem," *National Parliamentarian*, Second Quarter 2012, 19–24.

40. For the development of these points, see Jon L. Ericson, "Limit or Extend Limits of Debate: Another Motion to Be Eliminated?" *Parliamentary Journal* 31 (July 1990), 84–87. See also Schlotzhauer, Evans, and Stipp, *Parliamentary Opinions*, 32, question 69.

41. Robert, Evans, and Keesey, "The Rules," 6.

42. On what to call the motion, they are in less agreement. George Demeter

(*Demeter's Manual*, 92) and Lena LaNelle Hardcastle (*By the Rule*, 233) admit the phrase is misleading but retain it; Farwell (*Majority Rules*, 26, 47) prefers "vote immediately"; Keesey (*Modern Parliamentary Procedure*, 51), O. Garfield Jones (*Senior Manual for Group Leadership*, 23), Henry A. Davidson (*Handbook of Parliamentary Procedure*, 64), Hugo E. Hellman (*Parliamentary Procedure*, 40), and the *American Institute of Parliamentarians Standard Code of Parliamentary Procedure* use "close debate." The *Standard Code of Parliamentary Procedure* went from "vote immediately" (2nd edition, 67) to "close debate" (3rd edition, 58) to "close debate and vote immediately" (4th edition, revised by AIP, 65). For a history of the call for the previous question, a criticism of the term, and the arguments for one preference over another, see Henry A. Davidson, "The Previous History of the Previous Question," *Parliamentary Journal* 7 (Oct. 1966), 16–22 (but be forewarned that Davidson opens his article by saying "previous question" is "wretched" and concludes by saying that it has been "perverted"). See also T. Page Johnson, "Thomas Jefferson . . . and the Previous Question," *National Parliamentarian*, Fourth Quarter 1995, 32–37; Jim Slaughter, "The Previous Question: Origin and Development," *Parliamentary Journal* 34 (July 1993), 93–99; Margaret A. Banks, "The Previous Question, Closure, and the Modern Motion to Close Debate or Vote Immediately," *Parliamentary Journal* 19 (Jan. 1978), 32–36; Whitney G. Sampson, "The Previous Question," *Parliamentary Journal* 13 (Apr. 1972), 19–24; and Robert Luce, *Legislative Procedure*, 238–69.

43. *The Standard Code*, 4th edition, 66; *Standard Code AIP*, 68.

44. See, for example, Virginia Schlotzhauer, Floyd M. Riddick, and John R. Stipp, "Parliamentary Opinions," *Parliamentary Journal* 29 (Apr. 1988), 62, question 88–258, or Virginia Schlotzhauer, Margaret A. Banks, Floyd M. Riddick, and John R. Stipp, *Parliamentary Opinions II: Solutions to Problems of Organizations* (Dubuque, Iowa: Kendall/Hunt, 1992), 27, question 37.

45. *The Standard Code*, 4th edition, 68. *Standard Code AIP* does not use the term *postpone temporarily*, but uses *Table (Dispose without a Direct Vote)*, which is undebatable and requires a two-thirds vote, 70.

46. *The Standard Code*, 4th edition requires a two-thirds vote for passage of the motion to table whenever its purpose is to prevent discussion of a motion and thus transfers bad advice into a bad rule. Under this rule, the chair states, "The Chair interprets the motion to table as motion to kill the motion without further debate, and thus a two-thirds vote is required," 70. The chair has enough problems without alleging the motive of a member. For a review of the difficulty in asking the chair to decide between majority or two-thirds vote, see H. W. Hildebrandt, "The Two-Thirds Vote and the Motion to Table," *Parliamentary Journal* 17 (Jan. 1976), 32–36. An example of how the motion to Postpone is preferable to the motion to Lay on the Table is offered in John D. Stackpole, Margaret A. Banks, and Michael E. Malamut, "Parliamentary Opinions" in *Parliamentary Journal* 44 (Jan. 2003), 39–40, question 2003-489.

47. Gregg Phifer in "A Dialogue: The Statement Table the Motion?" *Parliamentary Journal* 25 (Oct. 1984), 124–28, and "Dialogue: A Response to the Response," *Parliamentary Journal* 25 (Oct. 1984), 132, attacks, and Edwin C. Bliss in "A Dialogue: The Response Table the Motion?—Another View," *Parliamentary Journal* 25 (Oct. 1984), 128–32, defends (kind of) the motion. Even an article by Hugo Hellman and Byrl A. Whitney, "In Defense of Tabling" (*Parliamentary Journal* 6 (Oct. 1965), 19–22) is not a defense of tabling. Those who wish to eliminate the motion are told to back off by Tom Sarbeck, "If It Ain't Broke, Don't Fix It: The Motion to Table," *Parliamentary Journal* 26 (Jan. 1985), 11–14.

48. Demeter, *Demeter's Manual*, 106, 109.

49. Hardcastle, *By the Rule*, 220.

50. Virginia Schlotzhauer, William J. Evans, and John R. Stipp, "Parliamentary Opinions," *Parliamentary Journal* 17 (July 1976), 44, question 76–34.

51. See, for example, *The Standard Code*, 4th edition, 77, and *Standard Code AIP*, 77.

52. *Robert's* stipulation that the motion to adjourn is privileged, even if no business is pending, is an exception to the general rule that privileged motions lose their privileged status when no business is pending (233–34).

53. Marshall Soren, Robert W. English, and Charles Greenstein, "Opinions," *Parliamentary Journal* 12 (Oct. 1971), 27–29, question 71–16.

54. For a different answer, see Soren, English, and Greenstein, "Opinions," 29, question 71–18, "Criticism Outside Meetings."

55. John D. Stackpole, "Suspending the Rules 'in the Face of . . . a Minority,'" *National Parliamentarian*, Second Quarter 2001, 33–34.

56. *The Standard Code*, 4th edition, 86; *Standard Code AIP*, 87–88. The name is based on the legend of the Gordian Knot, which foretold that whoever untied the knot would rule all of Asia. Alexander the Great solved the problem in 333 B.C. by cutting through the knot with his sword. According to Hy Farwell, the "Gordian Knot" purpose of suspending the rules was introduced by Floyd Riddick, parliamentarian emeritus of the United States Senate, at a meeting of the board of directors of the American Institute of Parliamentarians. Herman W. Farwell, *Point of Opinion* (West Conshohocken, Pa.: Infinity, 2005), 27.

57. Seeking clarification from other texts, Hardcastle (*By the Rule*, 23, 24), and Sturgis (*The Standard Code*, 2nd edition, 89) tend toward restatement of *Robert's*. Translating into language every delegate can understand, Hugo E. Hellman (*Parliamentary Procedure*) says it can be used to prevent motions that are "just plain stupid," 59. Zoe Steen Moore and John B. Moore (*Essentials of Parliamentary Procedure*) and George Demeter (*Demeter's Manual*) are more specific. Moore and Moore state that the purpose is to prevent consideration of "a motion calling for unnecessary or hasty action on a highly *controversial* question that may sometimes be very embarrassing," 60. Demeter does the best job: "Objection to the consideration of a question is used when an original

main motion is of a delicate or personal nature, or is contentious or inflamma-
tory (such as sectarian, political, racial, etc.), or is irrelevant, unprofitable, or
otherwise objectionable or discriminatory," 141. Davidson does not bother with
specific reasons for the motion and thus plants the seed for abuse. He begins,
"One of an organization's precious rights is its privilege to refuse to consider the
matter," and then includes an unfortunate sentence: "No matter what the reason,
if two-thirds of the members present do not want to consider a matter, it will
not be considered" (*Handbook of Parliamentary Procedure*, 14). *The Standard
Code*, 4th edition eliminates the motion, 233–34; Floyd M. Riddick and Miriam
H. Butcher (*Riddick's Rules of Procedure*) ignore it. For another review of the
question, see Schlotzhauer, Banks, Riddick, and Stipp, *Parliamentary Opinions
II,* 33, question 44.

58. Schlotzhauer, Evans, and Stipp, *Parliamentary Opinions*, 52, question 109.

59. Demeter, *Demeter's Manual*, 138. On a voice vote it may be difficult for
members to hear the magnitude of voices outside their immediate area, especially in conventions. A Division can give the chair and members a better sense
of the voting.

60. For a concise review of parliamentary authorities on Division of the
Assembly, see Schlotzhauer et al., "Parliamentary Opinions," *Parliamentary
Journal* 19 (Oct. 1978), 20, 21, question 78–82.

61. For an example, see Schlotzhauer et al., "Parliamentary Opinions," *Parliamentary Journal* 18 (Oct. 1977), 32, question 77–62.

62. The problem is addressed in Schlotzhauer et al., "Parliamentary Opinions," *Parliamentary Journal* 17 (July 1976), 44, question 76–35, and in Schlotzhauer, Evans, and Stipp, *Parliamentary Opinions*, 52–53, question 110.

63. The question is raised in the *Parliamentary Journal—with* two different
answers. See "Opinions," *Parliamentary Journal* 5 (Jan. 1964), 32, question 4;
and Arthur J. Fear, "New Opinion on 'Withdrawal of Petition,'" *Parliamentary
Journal* 5 (Apr. 1964), 38.

64. Moving to rescind at the same meeting involves several technicalities. See
Jon L. Ericson, "Rescind: How Soon May the Motion Be Made?" *Parliamentary
Journal* 31 (Oct. 1990), 110–14.

65. *The Standard Code*, 4th edition, 40–41. See also *Standard Code AIP*, 46.

66. Keesey (*Modern Parliamentary Procedure*, 76), Farwell (*Majority Rules*,
42), and Riddick and Butcher (*Riddick's Rules*, 166) agree with Sturgis and with
the authors of *Robert's* 3rd edition (34, 37) and 4th edition (38, 42). For other
examples of positions critical of *Robert's*, see John M. Burt, "Parliamentary
Procedure as Law," *Parliamentary Journal* 15 (July 1974), 8–12; Whitney Sampson,
"Of Reconsideration," *Parliamentary Journal* 11 (July 1971), 17–22; and Edwin C.
Bliss, "Reconsideration: A Summing Up," *Parliamentary Journal* 28 (Oct. 1987),
130–33. For examples of those in agreement with *Robert's*, see Wayne E. Hoogestraat, "The Logic of *Robert's* Restricted Eligibility for Moving Reconsideration,"

Parliamentary Journal 15 (Oct. 1974), 25–26; George Demeter, "Some Significant Aspects on Reconsideration," *Parliamentary Journal* 14 (Jan. 1973), 9–12; J. David Lofton, "Must One Prevail to Change One's Mind? The Courts' Treatment of the Motion to Reconsider," *Parliamentary Journal* 28 (July 1987), 101–5; and William Dixon Southworth, "Some Considerations of Reconsideration," *Parliamentary Journal* 28 (July 1987), 105–7.

67. For the argument that the problem in large conventions could be lessened by increasing the number of delegates required to submit a new business item, see Jon Ericson, "Misunderstanding Democracy: How Many Delegates Does It Take to Move a Motion?" *Parliamentary Journal* 44 (Apr. 2003), 57–63. For an excellent exchange over reconsidering more than a single main motion at a time, see Michael E. Malamut, "Clinching, Mass Reconsideration, and Superclinching—Can They Really Do That?" *Parliamentary Journal* 40 (Jan. 1999), 1–18, and Hugh Cannon, "Superclinching? Yes, They Really Can Do That: Sometimes They Have To," *Parliamentary Journal* 41 (Jan. 2000), 1–5.

68. If a proviso establishes a later time for the amendment to go into effect, some parliamentary authorities argue that an affirmative vote may be reconsidered. For a brief but excellent review of the question see Thais M. Plaisted, "The Proviso: An Enigma," *Parliamentary Journal* 19 (July 1978), 27–28. See also Schlotzhauer et al., "Parliamentary Opinions," *Parliamentary Journal* 18 (July 1977), 32, question 56; and 19 (Apr. 1978), 27–31, question 69; and Schlotzhauer, Evans, and Stipp, *Parliamentary Opinions*, 65–70, question 23.

69. Those arguing to abolish the motion include *The Standard Code*, 4th edition, 237; Keesey, *Modern Parliamentary Procedure*, 91; English, *Modern Code*, 4; and Darwin Patnode, "Reconsideration," *Parliamentary Journal* 20 (Apr. 1979), 43–44. Also, for retaining the motion as one of those rarely used "arrows in the quiver of the parliamentarian," see William Dixon Southworth, "The Oddest One of All Motions: Reconsider and Enter on the Minutes," *Parliamentary Journal* 44 (Apr. 2003), 65–67.

Part IV

70. See Model Nonprofit Corporation Act Subcommittee, Committee on Nonprofit Organizations, ABA Section of Business Law, "Changes in the Model Nonprofit Corporation Act—Miscellaneous and Technical Amendments," *Business Lawyer* 67 (Feb. 2012), 473–89; Michael E. Malamut, "District of Columbia Enacts Member-Friendly Nonprofit Corporation Law, Part I," *National Parliamentarian*, Second Quarter 2011, 11–15; Michael E. Malamut, "District of Columbia Enacts Member-Friendly Nonprofit Corporation Law, Part II," *National Parliamentarian*, Third Quarter 2011, 30–35; Michael E. Malamut, "District of Columbia Enacts Member-Friendly Nonprofit Corporation Law, Part III," *National Parliamentarian*, Fourth Quarter 2011, 8–12; Michael E. Malamut, "Issues of Concern to Parliamentarians Raised by the 2008 Revision of the Model

Nonprofit Corporation Act," *National Parliamentarian*, First Quarter 2009, 24–31; Michael E. Malamut, "Issues of Concern to Parliamentarians Raised by the 1952 Model Nonprofit Corporation Act," *National Parliamentarian*, Third Quarter 2008, 16–21; James H. Slaughter, "Statutes and Procedures of Community Associations," *National Parliamentarian*, First Quarter 2005, 9–18; James H. Slaughter, "Avoid the Practice of Law," First Quarter 2003, 16–18; James H. Slaughter, "Community Associations and the Parliamentarian," *National Parliamentarian*, First Quarter 2000, 25–28.

71. George S. Hills, *Managing Corporate Meetings: A Legal and Procedural Guide* (New York: Ronald Press, 1977), and Thais M. Plaisted, "The Quorum," *Parliamentary Journal* 6 (Oct. 1965), 10, agree. Hills says, "a quorum consisting of a simple majority of a collective body of a fixed number is not affected by vacancies or by self-disqualification of members so long as a quorum consisting of a majority of the whole body is present" (141). Plaisted writes, "Failure to fill a vacancy on a board or committee requiring a specific membership does not reduce the quorum." George Demeter and "Opinions," *Parliamentary Journal* 8 (Oct. 1967), 30, disagree. Demeter says, "Members dead, disqualified, refusing to qualify or who have not yet been sworn or have resigned or been suspended or expelled are *not* counted as *members* of the body, and hence they are not computed in determining its majority quorum requirement" (*Demeter's Manual*, 151). And, according to "Opinions," "The bylaws call for a board of fourteen, but there were two vacancies. At this meeting there were seven present. Was there a quorum? Ans. Yes, under common law and no bylaw providing for less. In this case the board consists of twelve until the vacancies are filled. A majority (the natural quorum) is seven." *Robert's* does not address the question.

72. Demeter, *Demeter's Manual*, 92, 309. Again, *Robert's* does not address the question. See Burt, "Parliamentary Procedure as Law," 10–12: "Robert . . . is not clear on this matter."

73. For a review of parliamentary authorities, see Schlotzhauer et al., *Parliamentary Opinions,* 82–83, question 158.

74. James H. Slaughter, "Statutes and Procedures of Community Associations," *National Parliamentarian*, First Quarter 2005, 9–18; James H. Slaughter, "Community Associations and the Parliamentarian," *National Parliamentarian*, First Quarter 2000, 25–28.

75. This language is slightly modified from the 10th edition (which made clear that only motions allowed in the absence of a quorum are permitted). The addition of "the conduct of the meeting before its adoption" is not further defined and could lead to trouble, as it suggests that even motions to adopt rules governing consideration of the Credentials Committee might be in order prior to the report. With the membership of the convention not yet resolved, such additional motions could easily bring the convention to a stop before it has started.

76. Nancy Sylvester, *The Complete Idiot's Guide to Robert's Rules*, 2nd ed. (New York: Penguin, 2010), 227.

77. *Robert's* recommended language simply has the chair declare the minutes approved when no one responds to the question "Are there any corrections?" (355). Asking the follow-up question, "Is there objection to approving the minutes?," involves members in the process and is less likely to lead to procedural confusion.

78. Megan Hawkins, "Presidential race to have runoff; Fung and Hanson victorious," *The Times-Delphic*, 22 Feb. 2002, 1. Also, in the 2000 election for National Education Association Student Program President, Candidate A received 35 votes out of 69 votes cast. The organization's bylaws stated that a candidate must receive majority (50 percent plus 1) in order to be declared the winner. Half of 69 is 34.5. One more than half of 34.5 is 35.5. A lesson learned: The organization amended its bylaws by striking "50% plus 1." For yet another example, see Schlotzhauer et al., "Parliamentary Opinions," *Parliamentary Journal* 26 (July 1985), 116–17, question 85–154, 208, or Schlotzhauer et al, *Parliamentary Opinions II*, 53, question 66. The bylaws defined majority as 51 percent, and the vote was fifty-one to fifty: motion rejected. See also, Kim Goldsworthy, "The Great Myth: Fifty Plus One," *Parliamentary Journal* 45 (Oct. 2004), 130–34.

79. Even experienced parliamentarians can benefit from a review of the sometimes complex situations involving voting. See Schlotzhauer et al., *Parliamentary Opinions II*, 49–58, questions 60–73; Lochrie, *Meeting Procedures*, 129–49.

80. Demeter, *Demeter's Manual*, 35-36.

81. *The Standard Code*, 4th edition, 134. Riddick and Butcher *(Riddick's Rules,* 101–2, 205) follow Sturgis, while Hills *(Corporate Meetings,* 131–32) and Demeter *(Demeter's Manual,* 247–50, 310) reflect the traditional definition found in *Robert's*. For examples of how to handle illegal votes, see Schlotzhauer et al., *Parliamentary Opinions,* 89, question 169; and 114–15, questions 206 and 207; and Schlotzhauer et al., *Parliamentary Opinions II,* 65–66, questions 83 and 84; and Stackpole et al, "Parliamentary Opinions," *Parliamentary Journal* 41 (Oct. 2000), 128–29.

82. See Schlotzhauer et al., *Parliamentary Opinions II,* 49–50, question 61.

83. Michael E. Malamut, "Issues of Concern to Parliamentarians Raised by the 2008 Revision of the Model Nonprofit Corporation Act," *National Parliamentarian,* First Quarter 2009, 24–31.

84. *The Standard Code*, 4th edition, 131; also see *Standard Code AIP,* 136.

85. The requirement of a supermajority vote deserves careful attention. See Jon Ericson, "Super Majority: Super Democratic—or Simply Undemocratic?" *Parliamentary Journal* 35 (Apr. 1994), 43–46; and rejoinders, Tom Sarbeck, "The Supermajority Debate: A Variation on a Theme," *Parliamentary Journal* 35 (July 1994), 81–82, and Edwin C. Bliss, "The Supermajority Supercontroversy," *Parliamentary Journal* 35 (Oct. 1994), 141–42. For the case for supermajority voting,

see John O. McGinnis and Michael B. Rappaport, "The Case for Supermajority Rules," *Policy Review* no. 98 (Dec. 1999–Jan. 2000), 45–59. See also Paul McClintock, "Muddled Meaning of Majority," *Parliamentary Journal* 46 (Jan. 2005), 25–26. Some authorities, such as *Mason's Manual*, avoid the question by requiring only a majority for procedural motions, including closing debate or suspending the rules.

86. For a discussion of online meeting issues, see Nancy Sylvester, "E-Meetings: Pitfalls, Benefits, and Lessons Learned," *National Parliamentarian*, Fourth Quarter 2006, 6–11; see also the Electronic Unit of the National Association of Parliamentarians (eNAP) at https://sites.google.com/site/enapunit/. See also John D. Stackpole, "Rules for Electronic (e-mail) Meetings, or The E-liberative Assembly," *Parliamentary Journal* 46 (July 2001), 81–95.

87. See Schlotzhauer et al., *Parliamentary Opinions*, 13, question 204.

88. See Schlotzhauer et al., "Parliamentary Opinions," *Parliamentary Journal* 24 (Apr. 1983), 71, question 83–176. Members may not change their votes if the vote was by secret ballot, as there is no way of knowing how the member voted. See Schlotzhauer et al., "Parliamentary Opinions," *Parliamentary Journal* 24 (July 1983), 115, question 83–181. Both questions are also in Schlotzhauer et al, *Parliamentary Opinions II*, 64 and 67, questions 81 and 87.

89. The answer was an addition in the 1981 and subsequent editions of *Robert's* and reflects an effort to provide a definitive answer to a difficult question. See Robert W. English et al., "Opinions," *Parliamentary Journal* 11 (Jan. 1970), 27, question 105, and (Apr. 1970), 25, question 2. For a discussion reflecting differences on where to draw the line, see Schlotzhauer et al., "Parliamentary Opinions," *Parliamentary Journal* 17 (Apr. 1976), 39, question 76–30. Finally, see Schlotzhauer et al, *Parliamentary Opinions II*, 61, question 78.

90. See Soren et al., "Opinions," *Parliamentary Journal* 12 (Oct. 1971), 29, question 71–17.

91. An additional exception can arise when the negative vote is "intrinsically irrelevant" (i.e., cannot alter the outcome), such as when "a vote of one-third of the members present" is required and the affirmative vote exceeds that threshold (45). Even in such instance, taking the negative vote is advised. Since those who have not yet voted include both negative votes and abstentions, determining the negative vote can help gauge opposition numbers.

92. Schlotzhauer et al, *Parliamentary Opinions II*, 69–70, question 90.

93. For a discussion of various techniques of preferential voting, see Rachel T. Hare-Mustin, "A Second Look: Preferential Voting Systems," *Parliamentary Journal* 36 (July 1995), 109–17; James Lochrie, *Meeting Procedures: Parliamentary Law and Rules of Order for the 21st Century* (Lanham, Md.: Scarecrow Press, 2003); American Institute of Parliamentarians, *American Institute of Parliamentarians Standard Code of Parliamentary Procedure* (New York: McGraw

Hill, 2012).

94. Demeter, *Demeter's Manual*, 248.

95. See Schlotzhauer et al., *Parliamentary Opinions II*, 132, question 176.

96. See Schlotzhauer et al., *Parliamentary Opinions II*, 134, question 179.

97. Hugh Cannon, *Cannon's Concise Guide to Rules of Order* (Boston: Houghton Mifflin Co., 1992), preface, xix–xx. The benefits of good presiding skills are reflected in a story about Henry Martyn Robert in Ralph S. Smedley's *The Great Peacemaker*, 46:

> A Chicago man, visiting the office of the S. C. Griggs Company, remarked that he would very much like to see Major Robert in action, conducting a meeting.
>
> Mr. Griggs suggested that Major Robert was to preside at a large church convention in Milwaukee, and that the gentleman might do well to attend as an observer.
>
> A few days later, Mr. Griggs met the man again and asked, "Did you go up to Milwaukee to see Robert preside?"
>
> "Yes, I did," was the answer, in a rather disgusted tone.
>
> "What's the matter?" asked Mr. Griggs. "Didn't things go smoothly?"
>
> "Yes," said the other. "I went all the way to Milwaukee to see how this man Robert would get himself out of a jam. The whole thing went so smoothly that there was just nothing to see."

See also Thomas R. Duncan, "Participation Rights of the President," *Parliamentary Journal* 45 (Oct. 2004), 135–40.

98. See Schlotzhauer et al, *Parliamentary Opinions II*, 93, question 120. See Gene Bierbaum, *The Parliamentarian of Tomorrow* (Xlibris, 2010), 43–48; James "Jim" Jones, "Are Parliamentarians Becoming Extinct," *Parliamentary Journal* 51 (Jan. 2010), 25–28.

99. For example, see Hugh Cannon, "The Parliamentarian's Log-Cannon Format," *Parliamentary Journal* 40 (July 1999), 109–11.

100. Cannon, *Cannon's Concise Guide to Rules of Order*, 33–40.

101. Nancy Sylvester, *The Guerrilla Guide to Robert's Rules* (New York: Penguin, 2006), 143.

102. George Glover Crocker, *Principles of Procedure in Deliberative Bodies* (New York: G. P. Putnam's Sons, 1889), vii.

References

Abbate, Doris. "Greatest Flexibility—Creating and Filling a Blank." *Parliamentary Journal* 53 (Jan. 2012), 34-40.

American Institute of Parliamentarians. *American Institute of Parliamentarians Standard Code of Parliamentary Procedure*. New York: McGraw Hill, 2012.

———. *Readings in Parliamentary Law*. Dubuque, Iowa: Kendall/Hunt, 1992.

———. *The Standard Code of Parliamentary Procedure*, 4th ed. [Alice Sturgis]. New York: McGraw-Hill, 2001.

Banks, Margaret A. "The Previous Question, Closure, and the Modern Motion to Close Debate or Vote Immediately." *Parliamentary Journal* 19 (Jan. 1978), 32–36.

Bierbaum, Gene. *The Parliamentarian of Tomorrow*. Xlibris, 2010.

Bliss, Edwin C. "A Dialogue: The Response Table the Motion?—Another View." *Parliamentary Journal* 25 (Oct. 1984), 128–32.

———. "Reconsideration: A Summing Up." *Parliamentary Journal* 28 (Oct. 1987), 130–33.

———. "The Supermajority Supercontroversy." *Parliamentary Journal* 35 (Oct. 1994), 141–42.

———. "'User-Friendly' Parliamentary Procedure: A Rebuttal." *Parliamentary Journal* 33 (Apr. 1992), 78–80.

Bosmajian, Haig. *Readings in Parliamentary Procedure*. New York: Harper and Row, 1968.

Bridgman, Raymond L. "Parliamentary Law: A World Institution." *Bibliothecca Sacra* 66 (Oct. 1909), 650–60.

Burt, John M. "Parliamentary Procedure as Law." *Parliamentary Journal* 15 (July 1974), 8–13.

Callaghan, J. Calvin. "Precedence in Parliamentary Motions." *Parliamentary Journal* 7 (Apr. 1966), 21–26.

Cannon, Hugh. *Cannon's Concise Guide to Rules of Order*. Boston: Houghton Mifflin, 1992.

———. "The Parliamentarian's Log-Cannon Format." *Parliamentary Journal* 40 (July 1999), 109–11.

———. "Superclinching? Yes, They Really Can Do That: Sometimes They Have To." *Parliamentary Journal* 41 (Jan. 2000), 1–5.

Cleary, James W. "A Commentary on *Robert's Rules of Order Newly Revised*."

Parliamentary Journal 9 (Apr. 1968), 3–9.

Collins, Jeannette. "Opinions." *Parliamentary Journal* 10 (Apr. 1969), 30–32.

Crocker, George Glover. *Principles of Procedure in Deliberative Bodies.* New York: G. P. Putnam's Sons, 1889.

Dahms, Lester L. "The Importance of a Quorum." *Parliamentary Journal* 20 (Oct. 1979), 11–16.

Davidson, Henry A. "General Robert Rode a Buggy." *Parliamentary Journal* 7 (Jan. 1966), 8–12.

———. *Handbook of Parliamentary Procedure.* New York: Ronald Press, 1968.

——— "Let's Modernize Parliamentary Terminology." *Parliamentary Journal* 2 (Jan. 1962), 3–10.

———. "The Previous History of the Previous Question." *Parliamentary Journal* 7 (Oct. 1966), 16–22.

———. "Towards a More Informal Procedure." *Parliamentary Journal* 12 (Jan. 1971), 10, 31.

Demeter, George. *Demeter's Manual of Parliamentary Law and Procedure.* Boston: Little, Brown, 1969.

———. "Resolutions Can Circumvent Main Motion." *Parliamentary Journal* 13 (Jan. 1972), 25.

———. "Some Significant Aspects on Reconsideration." *Parliamentary Journal* 14 (Jan. 1973), 9–12.

———. "Twenty-Six Subsidiary Motions Pending at Once." *Parliamentary Journal* 12 (July 1971), 16 (reprinted in *Parliamentary Journal* 52 (Apr. 2011), 80).

Duncan, Marjorie H. "More on Filling Blanks." *Parliamentary Journal* 5 (Jan. 1964), 3–4.

Duncan, Thomas R. "Participation Rights of the President." *Parliamentary Journal* 45 (Oct. 2004), 135–40.

The Electronic Unit of the National Association of Parliamentarians (eNAP), https://sites.google.com/site/enapunit/.

Emery, Emogene. "AIP's Response *to RONR.*" *Parliamentary Journal* 12 (Apr. 1971), 8–11.

English, Robert W. "Modern Code Governing Motions." Unpublished ms., 1960 (available from authors).

———. "A New View of Subsidiary Motions." *Parliamentary Journal* 10 (Jan. 1969), 19–23.

English, Robert W., Rheva Oft Shryock, and Marshall Soren. "Opinions." *Parliamentary Journal* 11 (Jan. 1970), 25–30; and (Apr. 1970), 25–26.

Ericson, Jon L. "Limit or Extend Limits of Debate: Another Motion to Be Eliminated?" *Parliamentary Journal* 31 (July 1990), 84–87.

———. "Misunderstanding Democracy: How Many Delegates Does It Take to Move a Motion?" *Parliamentary Journal* 44 (April 2003), 57–63.

———. "Rescind: How Soon May the Motion Be Made?" *Parliamentary Journal* 31 (Oct. 1990), 110–14.

———. "Super Majority: Super Democratic—or Simply Undemocratic?" *Parliamentary Journal* 35 (Apr. 1994), 43–46.

Evans, William J. "Concerning *ROR* Newly Revised." *Parliamentary Journal* 10 (Oct. 1969), 3–13.

Farwell, Herman W. *The Majority Rules: A Manual of Procedure for Most Groups.* Pueblo, Colo.: High Publishers, 1980.

Fear, Arthur J. "New Opinion on 'Withdrawal of Petition.'" *Parliamentary Journal* 5 (Apr. 1964), 38.

Fishman, Donald. "The Elusive Henry Martyn Robert: A Historical Problem." *National Parliamentarian*, Second Quarter 2012, 19–24.

Gerber, Shmuel. "Rungs of the Ladder: Precedence of Subsidiary Motions." *Parliamentary Journal* 48 (July 2007), 98–107.

Glazer, Barry. "Negative Motion, No Motion, What Can We Do?" *Parliamentary Journal* 42 (Apr. 2011), 76–79.

Goldsworthy, Kim. "'All Opposed, Same Sign'"—What?" *Parliamentary Journal* 51 (Oct. 2010), 141–44.

———. "The Great Myth: Fifty Plus One." *Parliamentary Journal* 45 (Oct. 2004), 130–34.

Hardcastle, Lena LaNelle. *By the Rule: Parliamentary Law Motions Made Easy.* Garland, Tex.: Stuart Books, 1974.

Hare-Mustin, Rachel T. "A Second Look: Preferential Voting Systems." *Parliamentary Journal* 36 (July 1995), 109–17.

Hawkins, Megan, "Presidential race to have runoff; Fung and Hanson victorious," *The Times-Delphic* (Drake University, Des Moines, Iowa), 22 Feb. 2002, 1.

Hellman, Hugo E. *Parliamentary Procedure.* New York: Macmillan, 1966.

———. "Robert's Precedence Is Nonsense." *Parliamentary Journal* 12 (Apr. 1971), 3–7.

Hellman, Hugo E., Byrl A. Whitney, and Robert W. English. "In Defense of Tabling." *Parliamentary Journal* 6 (Oct. 1965), 19–22.

Hildebrandt, H. W. "The Two-Thirds Vote and the Motion to Table." *Parliamentary Journal* 17 (Jan. 1976), 32–36.

Hills, George S. *Managing Corporate Meetings: A Legal and Procedural Guide.* New York: Ronald Press, 1977.

Holzhaus, Dominic. "Whose Motion Is It Anyway?" *Parliamentary Journal* 50 (July 2012), 83-90.

Hoogestraat, Wayne E. "The Logic of Robert's Restricted Eligibility for Moving Consideration." *Parliamentary Journal* 15 (Oct. 1974), 25–26.

———. "Secondary Amendments to a Main Motion?" *Parliamentary Journal* 21 (July 1980), 32–33.

Jefferson, Thomas. *A Manual of Practice for the Use of the Senate of the United States.* Old Saybrook, CT: Applewood Books, 1993 (republished from the 1801 edition in cooperation with the Library of Congress).

Jennings, C. Alan. *Robert's Rules for Dummies.* Hoboken, N.J.: Wiley Publishing, 2005.

Johnson, T. Page. "Thomas Jefferson . . . and the Previous Question," *National Parliamentarian,* Fourth Quarter 1995, 32–37.

Jones, James "Jim." "Are Parliamentarians Becoming Extinct?" *Parliamentary Journal* 51 (Jan. 2010), 25–28.

Jones, O. Garfield. *Senior Manual for Group Leadership.* New York: Appleton, Century Crofts, 1949.

Kain, Richard S. "Analogy in the Teaching of Precedence." *Parliamentary Journal* 6 (Apr. 1965), 23–27.

Keesey, Ray E. *Modern Parliamentary Procedure.* Boston: Houghton Mifflin, 1974.

Lewis, Arthur T., and Henry M. Robert. *Robert's Rules Simplified.* Mineola, N.Y.: Dover Publications, 2006.

Lochrie, Jim. "American Institute of Parliamentarians Standard Code of Parliamentary Procedure." *Parliamentary Journal* 53 (Jan. 2012), 29–33.

———. *Meeting Procedures: Parliamentary Law and Rules of Order for the 21st Century.* Lanham, Md.: Scarecrow, 2003.

Lofton, J. David. "Must One Prevail to Change One's Mind? The Courts' Treatment of the Motion to Reconsider." *Parliamentary Journal* 28 (July 1987), 101–5.

Luce, Robert. *Legislative Procedure: Parliamentary Practices and the Course of Business in the Framing of Statutes.* Boston: Houghton Mifflin, 1922.

Malamut, Michael E., "Clinching, Mass Reconsideration, and Superclinching— Can They Really Do That?" *Parliamentary Journal* 40 (Jan. 1999), 1–18.

———. "District of Columbia Enacts Member-Friendly Nonprofit Corporation Law, Part I." *National Parliamentarian,* Second Quarter 2011, 11–15.

———. "District of Columbia Enacts Member-Friendly Nonprofit Corporation Law, Part II." *National Parliamentarian,* Third Quarter 2011, 30–35.

———. "District of Columbia Enacts Member-Friendly Nonprofit Corporation Law, Part III." *National Parliamentarian,* Fourth Quarter 2011, 8–12.

———. "Issues of Concern to Parliamentarians Raised by the 1952 Model Nonprofit Corporation Act." *National Parliamentarian,* Third Quarter 2008, 24–30.

———. "Issues of Concern to Parliamentarians Raised by the 2008 Revision of the Model Nonprofit Corporation Act." *National Parliamentarian,* First Quarter 2009, 24–31.

Mason, Paul. "The Legal Side of Parliamentary Procedure," in *Readings in Parliamentary Procedure*, ed. Haig A. Bosmajian (New York: Harper & Row, 1968), 42–55.

McClintock, Paul. "History of 'Aye' and 'No.'" *Parliamentary Journal* 51 (Jan. 2010), 35–37.

———. "Muddled Meaning of Majority." *Parliamentary Journal* 46 (Jan. 2005), 25–26.

McGinnis, John O., and Michael B. Rappaport, "The Case for Supermajority Rules." *Policy Review*, no. 98 (Dec. 1999–Jan. 2000), 45–59.

Model Nonprofit Corporation Act Subcommittee, Committee on Nonprofit Organizations, ABA Section of Business Law. "Changes in the Model Nonprofit Corporation Act—Miscellaneous and Technical Amendments." *Business Lawyer* 67 (Feb. 2012), 473–89.

Moore, Zoe Steen, and John B. Moore. *Essentials of Parliamentary Procedure.* New York: Harper & Brothers, 1944.

National Association of Parliamentarians. *Parliamentary Questions and Answers*, vol. 4. Independence, Mo.: National Association of Parliamentarians, 2010.

National Conference of State Legislatures. *Mason's Manual of Legislative Procedure.* Eagan, Minn.: West, 2010.

"Opinions." *Parliamentary Journal* 5 (Jan. 1964), 31–38; 6 (Jan. 1965), 29–37; 8 (Oct. 1967), 30–33; and 13 (July 1972), 22.

"Opinions on Parliamentary Questions." *Parliamentary Journal* 1 (Mar. 1960), 9–11.

Patnode, Darwin. "Criteria for Germaneness of Amendments." *Parliamentary Journal* 13 (Apr. 1972), 14–18.

———. "Opinions." *Parliamentary Journal* 14 (Jan. 1973), 20–21.

———. "Reconsideration." *Parliamentary Journal* 20 (Apr. 1979), 43–44.

Patnode, Darwin, A. R. D. Robertson, and Whitney G. Sampson. "Official Opinions on Parliamentary Rules." *Parliamentary Journal* 14 (July 1973), 12–13.

Phifer, Gregg. "A Dialogue: A Response to the Response." *Parliamentary Journal* 25 (Oct. 1984), 132.

———. "A Dialogue: The Statement Table the Motion?" *Parliamentary Journal* 25 (Oct. 1984), 124–28.

———. "Maybe Robert Is Not the Worst Choice, But . . ." *Parliamentary Journal* 33 (Apr. 1992), 66–74.

——— "The Robert Heirs Blew It." *Parliamentary Journal* 23 (July 1982), 81–91.

———. "Trends in Parliamentary Procedure: Future Form and Practice." *Parliamentary Journal* 28 (Apr. 1987), 59–66.

Plaisted, Thais M. "The Proviso: An Enigma." *Parliamentary Journal* 19 (July 1978), 27–28.

————. "The Quorum." *Parliamentary Journal* 6 (Oct. 1965), 7–11.

————. "The When, the Why, and the Where of the Second." *Parliamentary Journal* 19 (Oct. 1978), 16–17.

Riddick, Floyd M., and Miriam H. Butcher. *Riddick's Rules of Procedure: A Modern Guide to Faster and More Efficient Meetings.* New York: Charles Scribner's Sons, 1985.

Robert, Henry M. *Parliamentary Law.* New York: Century, 1923.

————. *Robert's Rules of Order Revised.* Chicago: Scott, Foresman, 1915.

Robert, Henry M., III. "Guiding Principles for Changes in New Editions of Robert's Rules of Order Newly Revised." *National Parliamentarian,* First Quarter 2012, 7–14.

————. "Revising RONR: What We Can and Cannot Do." *National Parliamentarian,* First Quarter 2007, 6–15.

Robert, Henry M., III, William J. Evans, Daniel H. Honemann, and Thomas J. Balch. *Robert's Rules of Order Newly Revised.* 10th ed. Cambridge, Mass.: Da Capo Press, 2000.

Robert, Henry M., III, William J. Evans, and Ray E. Keesey. "The Rules: Can They Cope?" *Parliamentary Journal* 12 (Jan. 1971), 3–10.

Robert, Henry M., III, Daniel H. Honemann, and Thomas J. Balch. *Robert's Rules of Order Newly Revised.* 11th ed. Philadelphia: Da Capo Press, 2011.

————. *Robert's Rules of Order Newly Revised: In Brief.* 2nd ed. Philadelphia: Da Capo Press, 2011.

Robert, Sarah Corbin, Henry M. Robert III, James W. Cleary, and William J. Evans. *Robert's Rules of Order Newly Revised.* Glenview, Ill.: Scott, Foresman, 1970.

Robert, Sarah Corbin, Henry M. Robert III, and William J. Evans. *Robert's Rules of Order Newly Revised.* 9th ed. Glenview, Ill.: Scott, Foresman, 1990.

Sampson, Whitney G. "Of Reconsideration." *Parliamentary Journal* 12 (July 1971), 17–22.

————. "The Previous Question." *Parliamentary Journal* 13 (Apr. 1972), 19–24.

Sarbeck, Tom. "If It Ain't Broke, Don't Fix It: The Motion to Table." *Parliamentary Journal* 26 (Jan. 1985), 11–14.

————. "The Supermajority Debate: A Variation on a Theme." *Parliamentary Journal* 35 (July 1994), 81–82.

Schlotzhauer, Virginia, et al. "Parliamentary Opinions." *Parliamentary Journal* 17 (Apr. 1976), 39–42; (July 1976), 43–46.

————. "Parliamentary Opinions." *Parliamentary Journal* 18 (July 1977), 31–33; (Oct. 1977), 31–33.

————. "Parliamentary Opinions." *Parliamentary Journal* 19 (Apr. 1978), 27–30; (Oct. 1978), 18–21.

Schlotzhauer, Virginia, Margaret A. Banks, Floyd M. Riddick, and John R.

Stipp, *Parliamentary Opinions I1: Solutions to Problems of Organizations.* Dubuque, Iowa: Kendall/Hunt, 1992.

Schlotzhauer, Virginia, William J. Evans, and John R. Stipp. *Parliamentary Opinions: A Compilation and Revision of the Opinions Committee, 1958 to 1982.* Fort Wayne, Ind.: American Institute of Parliamentarians, 1982.

Schlotzhauer, Virginia, Floyd M. Riddick, and John R. Stipp. "Parliamentary Opinions." *Parliamentary Journal* 24 (Apr. 1983), 67–71; (July 1983), 112–15.

———. "Parliamentary Opinions." *Parliamentary Journal* 26 (July 1985), 114–17.

———. "Parliamentary Opinions." *Parliamentary Journal* 29 (Apr. 1988), 61–64.

Schlotzhauer, Virginia, and John R. Stipp. "Rebuttal." *Parliamentary Journal* 25 (Apr. 1984), 59–61.

Slaughter, Jim. "Avoid the Practice of Law." *National Parliamentarian,* First Quarter 2003, 16–18.

———. "Community Associations and the Parliamentarian." *National Parliamentarian,* First Quarter 2000, 25–28.

———. *The Complete Idiot's Guide to Parliamentary Procedure Fast-Track.* New York: Penguin, 2012.

———. "Parliamentary Practices of CPP's in 2000." *Parliamentary Journal* 42 (Jan. 2001), 1–11.

———. "The Previous Question: Origin and Development." *Parliamentary Journal* 34 (July 1993), 93–99.

———. "Statutes and Procedures of Community Associations." *National Parliamentarian,* First Quarter 2005, 9–14.

Smedley, Ralph S. *The Great Peacemaker.* Los Angeles: Bordon, 1955.

Smith, Mary D. "A Comparison between the Committee of the Whole and Its Alternate Forms in RONR." *Parliamentary Journal* 46 (July 2005), 112–17.

Soren, Marshall. *"Robert's Rules of Order Newly Revised*: A Review." *Parliamentary Journal* 11 (Apr. 1970), 17–20.

Soren, Marshall, Robert W. English, and Charles Greenstein. "Opinions." *Parliamentary Journal* 12 (Oct. 1971), 27–32.

Southworth, William Dixon. "Creating and Filling Blanks." *Parliamentary Journal* 34 (Apr. 1993), 71–74.

———. "The Oddest One of All Motions: Reconsider and Enter on the Minutes." *Parliamentary Journal* 44 (Apr. 2003), 65–67.

———. "Some Considerations of Reconsideration." *Parliamentary Journal* 28 (July 1987), 105–7.

Stackpole, John D. "Rules for Electronic (e-mail) Meetings or The E-liberative Assembly." *Parliamentary Journal* 42 (July 2001), 81–95.

———. "Suspending the Rules 'in the Face of . . . a Minority.'" *National Parliamentarian,* Second Quarter 2001, 33–34.

Stackpole, John D., Margaret A. Banks, and Michael E. Malamut. "Parliamentary

Opinions." *Parliamentary Journal* 44 (Jan. 2003), 37–40.

Stackpole, John D., Margaret A. Banks, and Virginia Schlotzhauer. "Parliamentary Opinions." *Parliamentary Journal* 41 (Oct. 2000), 128–32.

Sturgis, Alice. *Sturgis Standard Code of Parliamentary Procedure.* New York: McGraw-Hill, 1950.

———. *Sturgis Standard Code of Parliamentary Procedure.* 2nd ed. New York: McGraw-Hill, 1966.

———. *Sturgis Standard Code of Parliamentary Procedure,* 3rd ed. New York: McGraw-Hill, 1988.

Sullivan, John. "The Relevance of Robert's—The Virginia Experience." *Parliamentary Journal* 12 (Apr. 1971), 12–19.

Sylvester, Nancy. *The Complete Idiot's Guide to Robert's Rules.* 2nd ed. New York: Penguin, 2010.

———. "E-Meetings: Pitfalls, Benefits, and Lessons Learned." *National Parliamentarian,* Fourth Quarter 2006, 6–11.

———. *The Guerrilla Guide to Robert's Rules.* New York: Penguin, 2006.

———. "Robert Is the Only Choice." *Parliamentary Journal* 33 (Jan. 1992), 3–9.

Whitney, Byrl A. "'Filling Blanks': An Efficient Technique." *Parliamentary Journal* 5 (Oct. 1964), 7–11.

Zimmerman, Doris P. *Robert's Rules in Plain English.* 2nd ed. New York: HarperCollins, 2005.

Index

abstention, 126

accept versus adopt, committee reports, 40

acclamation, election by, 137

ad hoc committee, 34

Adjourn, 66, 67–69, 114
  Fix the Time to Which to, 69, 114
  qualified and unqualified form, 67

adjourned meeting, 69, 117–18

adopt versus accept, committee reports, 40

agenda, 48–49, 67, 70, 94, 119, 122

AIP. *See* American Institute of Parliamentarians

Amend, 23–28, 165*n*28
  bylaws, 26–27, 139–41
  committee reports, 38, 167*n*34
  and creating a blank, 31–33, 166*n*33
  debate on, 26, 29
  and Divide a Question, 84–85
  friendly, 26, 97
  germaneness, 24
  guideline for determining if a motion is amendable, 23
  hostile amendments, 24
  in order of precedence, 2–4, 161*n*15
  and Point of Order, 71
  and Postpone to a Certain Time, 46–47
  previous notice, 27
  and Previous Question (Close Debate), 55–56

primary and secondary, 25
  and Refer, 34–35
  and Rescind, 99–100
  and Substitute, 28–31
  and Suspend the Rules, 78
  vote required, 26
  See also bylaws

Amend Something Previously Adopted. *See* Rescind or Amend Something Previously Adopted

American Institute of Parliamentarians (AIP), 155, 159*n*3, 160*n*4

announcements, 7, 12, 64–65, 136–37

annual meeting, 118, 122–23

Appeal, 73–75, 144–45
  chair states question on, 74
  debate on, 73–74
  and Division of the Assembly, 88
  and Point of Order, 90–91, 115

approve committee report. *See* accept versus adopt, committee reports

assessments beyond dues, 129, 140

ballot vote, 78, 132, 135
  See also voting

blank, creating a, 31–33, 166*n*33

blank ballot, 126

boards
  chair participation, 143
  electronic meetings, 117
  ex officio member, 117
  informal procedures for smaller, 120–21
  nonmembers addressing, 11

185

Jim Slaughter is an attorney, a certified professional parliamentarian-teacher, a professional registered parliamentarian, and a past president of the American College of Parliamentary Lawyers. He is a partner in the North Carolina law firm of Rossabi Black Slaughter, PA.

Gaut Ragsdale, a certified professional parliamentarian-teacher and a registered parliamentarian, is a professor at Northern Kentucky University and associate dean of the College of Informatics.

Jon Ericson, the Ellis and Nelle Levitt Professor of Rhetoric and Communication Studies emeritus and a former provost at Drake University, is the original author of *Notes and Comments on "Robert's Rules."*

Parliamentary Motions

Motion	Second	Debatable	Amendable	Vote
PRIVILEGED MOTIONS				
Fix the Time to Which to Adjourn	Yes	No	Yes	Majority
Adjourn	Yes	No	No	Majority
Recess	Yes	No	Yes	Majority
Raise a Question of Privilege	No	No	No	None
SUBSIDIARY MOTIONS				
Lay on the Table	Yes	No	No	Majority
Previous Question (Close Debate)	Yes	No	No	2/3
Limit or Extend Limits of Debate	Yes	No	Yes	2/3
Postpone to a Certain Time	Yes	Yes	Yes	Majority
Commit or Refer	Yes	Yes	Yes	Majority
Amend the Amendment	Yes	Yes	No	Majority
Amend or Substitute	Yes	Yes	Yes	Majority
Postpone Indefinitely	Yes	Yes	No	Majority
MAIN MOTIONS				
Original				
Main Motion/Resolution	Yes	Yes	Yes	Majority
Bring a Question Again				
Reconsider	Yes	Varies	No	Majority
Take from the Table	Yes	No	No	Majority
Rescind	Yes	Yes	Yes	Majority with notice
INCIDENTAL MOTIONS				
No order of precedence				
Point of Order	No	No	No	None
Appeal	Yes	Varies	No	Majority
Suspend the Rules	Yes	No	No	2/3
Object to Consideration	No	No	No	2/3
Division of a Question	Yes	No	Yes	Majority
Division of the Assembly	No	No	No	None
Parliamentary Inquiry	No	No	No	None
Request for Information	No	No	No	None
Withdraw or Modify a Motion	No	No	No	Majority

Parliamentary Motions, Simplified

The following motions are listed in order of precedence. A motion can be introduced if it is higher on the list than the pending motion.

Motion	Debatable	Amendable	Vote
Adjourn	No	No	Majority
Recess	No	Yes	Majority
Previous Question (Close Debate)	No	No	2/3
Postpone	Yes	Yes	Majority
Refer	Yes	Yes	Majority
Amend the Amendment	Yes	No	Majority
Amend or Substitute	Yes	Yes	Majority
Main Motion/Resolution	Yes	Yes	Majority

Motions dealing with the general conduct of the meeting
No order of precedence

Motion	Debatable	Amendable	Vote
Point of Order	No	No	None
Appeal	Yes	No	Majority
Suspend the Rules	No	No	2/3
Division of a Question	No	Yes	Majority
Division of the Assembly	No	No	None
Parliamentary Inquiry	No	No	None
Request for Information	No	No	None
Withdraw or Modify a Motion	No	No	Majority

See ***Notes and Comments on "Robert's Rules,"*** fourth edition.

To obtain these charts in an electronic version or as a pocket-sized, laminated card, call (800) 621-2736 or go to www.siupress.com, enter Parliamentary in search.

Southern Illinois University Press